Series 63
Exam Secrets
Study Guide

DEAR FUTURE EXAM SUCCESS STORY

First of all, **THANK YOU** for purchasing Mometrix study materials!

Second, congratulations! You are one of the few determined test-takers who are committed to doing whatever it takes to excel on your exam. **You have come to the right place.** We developed these study materials with one goal in mind: to deliver you the information you need in a format that's concise and easy to use.

In addition to optimizing your guide for the content of the test, we've outlined our recommended steps for breaking down the preparation process into small, attainable goals so you can make sure you stay on track.

We've also analyzed the entire test-taking process, identifying the most common pitfalls and showing how you can overcome them and be ready for any curveball the test throws you.

Standardized testing is one of the biggest obstacles on your road to success, which only increases the importance of doing well in the high-pressure, high-stakes environment of test day. Your results on this test could have a significant impact on your future, and this guide provides the information and practical advice to help you achieve your full potential on test day.

Your success is our success

We would love to hear from you! If you would like to share the story of your exam success or if you have any questions or comments in regard to our products, please contact us at **800-673-8175** or **support@mometrix.com**.

Thanks again for your business and we wish you continued success!

Sincerely,
The Mometrix Test Preparation Team

> **Need more help? Check out our flashcards at:**
> **http://MometrixFlashcards.com/Series63**

TABLE OF CONTENTS

Introduction

Thank you for purchasing this resource! You have made the choice to prepare yourself for a test that could have a huge impact on your future, and this guide is designed to help you be fully ready for test day. Obviously, it's important to have a solid understanding of the test material, but you also need to be prepared for the unique environment and stressors of the test, so that you can perform to the best of your abilities.

For this purpose, the first section that appears in this guide is the **Secret Keys**. We've devoted countless hours to meticulously researching what works and what doesn't, and we've boiled down our findings to the five most impactful steps you can take to improve your performance on the test. We start at the beginning with study planning and move through the preparation process, all the way to the testing strategies that will help you get the most out of what you know when you're finally sitting in front of the test.

We recommend that you start preparing for your test as far in advance as possible. However, if you've bought this guide as a last-minute study resource and only have a few days before your test, we recommend that you skip over the first two Secret Keys since they address a long-term study plan.

If you struggle with **test anxiety**, we strongly encourage you to check out our recommendations for how you can overcome it. Test anxiety is a formidable foe, but it can be beaten, and we want to make sure you have the tools you need to defeat it.

Secret Key 1: Plan Big, Study Small

There's a lot riding on your performance. If you want to ace this test, you're going to need to keep your skills sharp and the material fresh in your mind. You need a plan that lets you review everything you need to know while still fitting in your schedule. We'll break this strategy down into three categories.

Information Organization

Start with the information you already have: the official test outline. From this, you can make a complete list of all the concepts you need to cover before the test. Organize these concepts into groups that can be studied together, and create a list of any related vocabulary you need to learn so you can brush up on any difficult terms. You'll want to keep this vocabulary list handy once you actually start studying since you may need to add to it along the way.

Time Management

Once you have your set of study concepts, decide how to spread them out over the time you have left before the test. Break your study plan into small, clear goals so you have a manageable task for each day and know exactly what you're doing. Then just focus on one small step at a time. When you manage your time this way, you don't need to spend hours at a time studying. Studying a small block of content for a short period each day helps you retain information better and avoid stressing over how much you have left to do. You can relax knowing that you have a plan to cover everything in time. In order for this strategy to be effective though, you have to start studying early and stick to your schedule. Avoid the exhaustion and futility that comes from last-minute cramming!

Study Environment

The environment you study in has a big impact on your learning. Studying in a coffee shop, while probably more enjoyable, is not likely to be as fruitful as studying in a quiet room. It's important to keep distractions to a minimum. You're only planning to study for a short block of time, so make the most of it. Don't pause to check your phone or get up to find a snack. It's also important to **avoid multitasking**. Research has consistently shown that multitasking will make your studying dramatically less effective. Your study area should also be comfortable and well-lit so you don't have the distraction of straining your eyes or sitting on an uncomfortable chair.

2

 The time of day you study is also important. You want to be rested and alert. Don't wait until just before bedtime. Study when you'll be most likely to comprehend and remember. Even better, if you know what time of day your test will be, set that time aside for study. That way your brain will be used to working on that subject at that specific time and you'll have a better chance of recalling information.

Finally, it can be helpful to team up with others who are studying for the same test. Your actual studying should be done in as isolated an environment as possible, but the work of organizing the information and setting up the study plan can be divided up. In between study sessions, you can discuss with your teammates the concepts that you're all studying and quiz each other on the details. Just be sure that your teammates are as serious about the test as you are. If you find that your study time is being replaced with social time, you might need to find a new team.

Secret Key 2: Make Your Studying Count

You're devoting a lot of time and effort to preparing for this test, so you want to be absolutely certain it will pay off. This means doing more than just reading the content and hoping you can remember it on test day. It's important to make every minute of study count. There are two main areas you can focus on to make your studying count.

Retention

It doesn't matter how much time you study if you can't remember the material. You need to make sure you are retaining the concepts. To check your retention of the information you're learning, try recalling it at later times with minimal prompting. Try carrying around flashcards and glance at one or two from time to time or ask a friend who's also studying for the test to quiz you.

To enhance your retention, look for ways to put the information into practice so that you can apply it rather than simply recalling it. If you're using the information in practical ways, it will be much easier to remember. Similarly, it helps to solidify a concept in your mind if you're not only reading it to yourself but also explaining it to someone else. Ask a friend to let you teach them about a concept you're a little shaky on (or speak aloud to an imaginary audience if necessary). As you try to summarize, define, give examples, and answer your friend's questions, you'll understand the concepts better and they will stay with you longer. Finally, step back for a big picture view and ask yourself how each piece of information fits with the whole subject. When you link the different concepts together and see them working together as a whole, it's easier to remember the individual components.

Finally, practice showing your work on any multi-step problems, even if you're just studying. Writing out each step you take to solve a problem will help solidify the process in your mind, and you'll be more likely to remember it during the test.

Modality

Modality simply refers to the means or method by which you study. Choosing a study modality that fits your own individual learning style is crucial. No two people learn best in exactly the same way, so it's important to know your strengths and use them to your advantage.

4

For example, if you learn best by visualization, focus on visualizing a concept in your mind and draw an image or a diagram. Try color-coding your notes, illustrating them, or creating symbols that will trigger your mind to recall a learned concept. If you learn best by hearing or discussing information, find a study partner who learns the same way or read aloud to yourself. Think about how to put the information in your own words. Imagine that you are giving a lecture on the topic and record yourself so you can listen to it later.

For any learning style, flashcards can be helpful. Organize the information so you can take advantage of spare moments to review. Underline key words or phrases. Use different colors for different categories. Mnemonic devices (such as creating a short list in which every item starts with the same letter) can also help with retention. Find what works best for you and use it to store the information in your mind most effectively and easily.

Secret Key 3: Practice the Right Way

Your success on test day depends not only on how many hours you put into preparing, but also on whether you prepared the right way. It's good to check along the way to see if your studying is paying off. One of the most effective ways to do this is by taking practice tests to evaluate your progress. Practice tests are useful because they show exactly where you need to improve. Every time you take a practice test, pay special attention to these three groups of questions:

- The questions you got wrong
- The questions you had to guess on, even if you guessed right
- The questions you found difficult or slow to work through

This will show you exactly what your weak areas are, and where you need to devote more study time. Ask yourself why each of these questions gave you trouble. Was it because you didn't understand the material? Was it because you didn't remember the vocabulary? Do you need more repetitions on this type of question to build speed and confidence? Dig into those questions and figure out how you can strengthen your weak areas as you go back to review the material.

 Additionally, many practice tests have a section explaining the answer choices. It can be tempting to read the explanation and think that you now have a good understanding of the concept. However, an explanation likely only covers part of the question's broader context. Even if the explanation makes perfect sense, **go back and investigate** every concept related to the question until you're positive you have a thorough understanding.

As you go along, keep in mind that the practice test is just that: practice. Memorizing these questions and answers will not be very helpful on the actual test because it is unlikely to have any of the same exact questions. If you only know the right answers to the sample questions, you won't be prepared for the real thing. **Study the concepts** until you understand them fully, and then you'll be able to answer any question that shows up on the test.

It's important to wait on the practice tests until you're ready. If you take a test on your first day of study, you may be overwhelmed by the amount of material covered and how much you need to learn. Work up to it gradually.

On test day, you'll need to be prepared for answering questions, managing your time, and using the test-taking strategies you've learned. It's a lot to balance, like a mental marathon that will have a big impact on your future. Like training for a marathon, you'll need to start slowly and work your way up. When test day arrives, you'll be ready.

6

Start with the strategies you've read in the first two Secret Keys—plan your course and study in the way that works best for you. If you have time, consider using multiple study resources to get different approaches to the same concepts. It can be helpful to see difficult concepts from more than one angle. Then find a good source for practice tests. Many times, the test website will suggest potential study resources or provide sample tests.

Practice Test Strategy

If you're able to find at least three practice tests, we recommend this strategy:

UNTIMED AND OPEN-BOOK PRACTICE

Take the first test with no time constraints and with your notes and study guide handy. Take your time and focus on applying the strategies you've learned.

TIMED AND OPEN-BOOK PRACTICE

Take the second practice test open-book as well, but set a timer and practice pacing yourself to finish in time.

TIMED AND CLOSED-BOOK PRACTICE

Take any other practice tests as if it were test day. Set a timer and put away your study materials. Sit at a table or desk in a quiet room, imagine yourself at the testing center, and answer questions as quickly and accurately as possible.

Keep repeating timed and closed-book tests on a regular basis until you run out of practice tests or it's time for the actual test. Your mind will be ready for the schedule and stress of test day, and you'll be able to focus on recalling the material you've learned.

Secret Key 4: Pace Yourself

Once you're fully prepared for the material on the test, your biggest challenge on test day will be managing your time. Just knowing that the clock is ticking can make you panic even if you have plenty of time left. Work on pacing yourself so you can build confidence against the time constraints of the exam. Pacing is a difficult skill to master, especially in a high-pressure environment, so **practice is vital**.

Set time expectations for your pace based on how much time is available. For example, if a section has 60 questions and the time limit is 30 minutes, you know you have to average 30 seconds or less per question in order to answer them all. Although 30 seconds is the hard limit, set 25 seconds per question as your goal, so you reserve extra time to spend on harder questions. When you budget extra time for the harder questions, you no longer have any reason to stress when those questions take longer to answer.

Don't let this time expectation distract you from working through the test at a calm, steady pace, but keep it in mind so you don't spend too much time on any one question. Recognize that taking extra time on one question you don't understand may keep you from answering two that you do understand later in the test. If your time limit for a question is up and you're still not sure of the answer, mark it and move on, and come back to it later if the time and the test format allow. If the testing format doesn't allow you to return to earlier questions, just make an educated guess; then put it out of your mind and move on.

On the easier questions, be careful not to rush. It may seem wise to hurry through them so you have more time for the challenging ones, but it's not worth missing one if you know the concept and just didn't take the time to read the question fully. Work efficiently but make sure you understand the question and have looked at all of the answer choices, since more than one may seem right at first.

Even if you're paying attention to the time, you may find yourself a little behind at some point. You should speed up to get back on track, but do so wisely. Don't panic; just take a few seconds less on each question until you're caught up. Don't guess without thinking, but do look through the answer choices and eliminate any you know are wrong. If you can get down to two choices, it is often worthwhile to guess from those. Once you've chosen an answer, move on and don't dwell on any that you skipped or had to hurry through. If a question was taking too long, chances are it was one of the harder ones, so you weren't as likely to get it right anyway.

On the other hand, if you find yourself getting ahead of schedule, it may be beneficial to slow down a little. The more quickly you work, the more likely you are to make a careless mistake that will affect your score. You've budgeted time for each question, so don't be afraid to spend that time. Practice an efficient but careful pace to get the most out of the time you have.

Secret Key 5: Have a Plan for Guessing

When you're taking the test, you may find yourself stuck on a question. Some of the answer choices seem better than others, but you don't see the one answer choice that is obviously correct. What do you do?

The scenario described above is very common, yet most test takers have not effectively prepared for it. Developing and practicing a plan for guessing may be one of the single most effective uses of your time as you get ready for the exam.

In developing your plan for guessing, there are three questions to address:

- When should you start the guessing process?
- How should you narrow down the choices?
- Which answer should you choose?

When to Start the Guessing Process

Unless your plan for guessing is to select C every time (which, despite its merits, is not what we recommend), you need to leave yourself enough time to apply your answer elimination strategies. Since you have a limited amount of time for each question, that means that if you're going to give yourself the best shot at guessing correctly, you have to decide quickly whether or not you will guess.

Of course, the best-case scenario is that you don't have to guess at all, so first, see if you can answer the question based on your knowledge of the subject and basic reasoning skills. Focus on the key words in the question and try to jog your memory of related topics. Give yourself a chance to bring the knowledge to mind, but once you realize that you don't have (or you can't access) the knowledge you need to answer the question, it's time to start the guessing process.

It's almost always better to start the guessing process too early than too late. It only takes a few seconds to remember something and answer the question from knowledge. Carefully eliminating wrong answer choices takes longer. Plus, going through the process of eliminating answer choices can actually help jog your memory.

Summary: Start the guessing process as soon as you decide that you can't answer the question based on your knowledge.

How to Narrow Down the Choices

The next chapter in this book (**Test-Taking Strategies**) includes a wide range of strategies for how to approach questions and how to look for answer choices to eliminate. You will definitely want to read those carefully, practice them, and figure out which ones work best for you. Here though, we're going to address a mindset rather than a particular strategy.

Your odds of guessing an answer correctly depend on how many options you are choosing from.

Number of options left	5	4	3	2	1
Odds of guessing correctly	20%	25%	33%	50%	100%

You can see from this chart just how valuable it is to be able to eliminate incorrect answers and make an educated guess, but there are two things that many test takers do that cause them to miss out on the benefits of guessing:

- Accidentally eliminating the correct answer
- Selecting an answer based on an impression

We'll look at the first one here, and the second one in the next section.

To avoid accidentally eliminating the correct answer, we recommend a thought exercise called **the $5 challenge**. In this challenge, you only eliminate an answer choice from contention if you are willing to bet $5 on it being wrong. Why $5? Five dollars is a small but not insignificant amount of money. It's an amount you could

afford to lose but wouldn't want to throw away. And while losing $5 once might not hurt too much, doing it twenty times will set you back $100. In the same way, each small decision you make—eliminating a choice here, guessing on a question there—won't by itself impact your score very much, but when you put them all together, they can make a big difference. By holding each answer choice elimination decision to a higher standard, you can reduce the risk of accidentally eliminating the correct answer.

The $5 challenge can also be applied in a positive sense: If you are willing to bet $5 that an answer choice *is* correct, go ahead and mark it as correct.

Summary: Only eliminate an answer choice if you are willing to bet $5 that it is wrong.

11

Which Answer to Choose

You're taking the test. You've run into a hard question and decided you'll have to guess. You've eliminated all the answer choices you're willing to bet $5 on. Now you have to pick an answer. Why do we even need to talk about this? Why can't you just pick whichever one you feel like when the time comes?

The answer to these questions is that if you don't come into the test with a plan, you'll rely on your impression to select an answer choice, and if you do that, you risk falling into a trap. The test writers know that everyone who takes their test will be guessing on some of the questions, so they intentionally write wrong answer choices to seem plausible. You still have to pick an answer though, and if the wrong answer choices are designed to look right, how can you ever be sure that you're not falling for their trap? The best solution we've found to this dilemma is to take the decision out of your hands entirely. Here is the process we recommend:

Once you've eliminated any choices that you are confident (willing to bet $5) are wrong, select the first remaining choice as your answer.

Whether you choose to select the first remaining choice, the second, or the last, the important thing is that you use some preselected standard. Using this approach guarantees that you will not be enticed into selecting an answer choice that looks right, because you are not basing your decision on how the answer choices look.

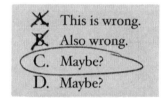

This is not meant to make you question your knowledge. Instead, it is to help you recognize the difference between your knowledge and your impressions. There's a huge difference between thinking an answer is right because of what you know, and thinking an answer is right because it looks or sounds like it should be right.

Summary: To ensure that your selection is appropriately random, make a predetermined selection from among all answer choices you have not eliminated.

Test-Taking Strategies

This section contains a list of test-taking strategies that you may find helpful as you work through the test. By taking what you know and applying logical thought, you can maximize your chances of answering any question correctly!

It is very important to realize that every question is different and every person is different: no single strategy will work on every question, and no single strategy will work for every person. That's why we've included all of them here, so you can try them out and determine which ones work best for different types of questions and which ones work best for you.

Question Strategies

⊘ READ CAREFULLY

Read the question and the answer choices carefully. Don't miss the question because you misread the terms. You have plenty of time to read each question thoroughly and make sure you understand what is being asked. Yet a happy medium must be attained, so don't waste too much time. You must read carefully and efficiently.

⊘ CONTEXTUAL CLUES

Look for contextual clues. If the question includes a word you are not familiar with, look at the immediate context for some indication of what the word might mean. Contextual clues can often give you all the information you need to decipher the meaning of an unfamiliar word. Even if you can't determine the meaning, you may be able to narrow down the possibilities enough to make a solid guess at the answer to the question.

⊘ PREFIXES

If you're having trouble with a word in the question or answer choices, try dissecting it. Take advantage of every clue that the word might include. Prefixes can be a huge help. Usually, they allow you to determine a basic meaning. *Pre-* means before, *post-* means after, *pro-* is positive, *de-* is negative. From prefixes, you can get an idea of the general meaning of the word and try to put it into context.

⊘ HEDGE WORDS

Watch out for critical hedge words, such as *likely, may, can, sometimes, often, almost, mostly, usually, generally, rarely,* and *sometimes.* Question writers insert these hedge phrases to cover every possibility. Often an answer choice will be wrong simply because it leaves no room for exception. Be on guard for answer choices that have definitive words such as *exactly* and *always.*

13

⊘ Switchback Words

Stay alert for *switchbacks*. These are the words and phrases frequently used to alert you to shifts in thought. The most common switchback words are *but*, *although*, and *however*. Others include *nevertheless*, *on the other hand*, *even though*, *while*, *in spite of*, *despite*, and *regardless of*. Switchback words are important to catch because they can change the direction of the question or an answer choice.

⊘ Face Value

When in doubt, use common sense. Accept the situation in the problem at face value. Don't read too much into it. These problems will not require you to make wild assumptions. If you have to go beyond creativity and warp time or space in order to have an answer choice fit the question, then you should move on and consider the other answer choices. These are normal problems rooted in reality. The applicable relationship or explanation may not be readily apparent, but it is there for you to figure out. Use your common sense to interpret anything that isn't clear.

Answer Choice Strategies

⊘ Answer Selection

The most thorough way to pick an answer choice is to identify and eliminate wrong answers until only one is left, then confirm it is the correct answer. Sometimes an answer choice may immediately seem right, but be careful. The test writers will usually put more than one reasonable answer choice on each question, so take a second to read all of them and make sure that the other choices are not equally obvious. As long as you have time left, it is better to read every answer choice than to pick the first one that looks right without checking the others.

⊘ Answer Choice Families

An answer choice family consists of two (in rare cases, three) answer choices that are very similar in construction and cannot all be true at the same time. If you see two answer choices that are direct opposites or parallels, one of them is usually the correct answer. For instance, if one answer choice says that quantity x increases and another either says that quantity x decreases (opposite) or says that quantity y increases (parallel), then those answer choices would fall into the same family. An answer choice that doesn't match the construction of the answer choice family is more likely to be incorrect. Most questions will not have answer choice families, but when they do appear, you should be prepared to recognize them.

⊘ Eliminate Answers

Eliminate answer choices as soon as you realize they are wrong, but make sure you consider all possibilities. If you are eliminating answer choices and realize that the last one you are left with is also wrong, don't panic. Start over and consider each choice again. There may be something you missed the first time that you will realize on the second pass.

⊘ Avoid Fact Traps

Don't be distracted by an answer choice that is factually true but doesn't answer the question. You are looking for the choice that answers the question. Stay focused on what the question is asking for so you don't accidentally pick an answer that is true but incorrect. Always go back to the question and make sure the answer choice you've selected actually answers the question and is not merely a true statement.

⊘ Extreme Statements

In general, you should avoid answers that put forth extreme actions as standard practice or proclaim controversial ideas as established fact. An answer choice that states the "process should be used in certain situations, if..." is much more likely to be correct than one that states the "process should be discontinued completely." The first is a calm rational statement and doesn't even make a definitive, uncompromising stance, using a hedge word *if* to provide wiggle room, whereas the second choice is far more extreme.

⊘ Benchmark

As you read through the answer choices and you come across one that seems to answer the question well, mentally select that answer choice. This is not your final answer, but it's the one that will help you evaluate the other answer choices. The one that you selected is your benchmark or standard for judging each of the other answer choices. Every other answer choice must be compared to your benchmark. That choice is correct until proven otherwise by another answer choice beating it. If you find a better answer, then that one becomes your new benchmark. Once you've decided that no other choice answers the question as well as your benchmark, you have your final answer.

⊘ Predict the Answer

Before you even start looking at the answer choices, it is often best to try to predict the answer. When you come up with the answer on your own, it is easier to avoid distractions and traps because you will know exactly what to look for. The right answer choice is unlikely to be word-for-word what you came up with, but it should be a close match. Even if you are confident that you have the right answer, you should still take the time to read each option before moving on.

General Strategies

⊘ Tough Questions

If you are stumped on a problem or it appears too hard or too difficult, don't waste time. Move on! Remember though, if you can quickly check for obviously incorrect answer choices, your chances of guessing correctly are greatly improved. Before you completely give up, at least try to knock out a couple of possible answers. Eliminate what you can and then guess at the remaining answer choices before moving on.

15

⊘ CHECK YOUR WORK

Since you will probably not know every term listed and the answer to every question, it is important that you get credit for the ones that you do know. Don't miss any questions through careless mistakes. If at all possible, try to take a second to look back over your answer selection and make sure you've selected the correct answer choice and haven't made a costly careless mistake (such as marking an answer choice that you didn't mean to mark). This quick double check should more than pay for itself in caught mistakes for the time it costs.

⊘ PACE YOURSELF

It's easy to be overwhelmed when you're looking at a page full of questions; your mind is confused and full of random thoughts, and the clock is ticking down faster than you would like. Calm down and maintain the pace that you have set for yourself. Especially as you get down to the last few minutes of the test, don't let the small numbers on the clock make you panic. As long as you are on track by monitoring your pace, you are guaranteed to have time for each question.

⊘ DON'T RUSH

It is very easy to make errors when you are in a hurry. Maintaining a fast pace in answering questions is pointless if it makes you miss questions that you would have gotten right otherwise. Test writers like to include distracting information and wrong answers that seem right. Taking a little extra time to avoid careless mistakes can make all the difference in your test score. Find a pace that allows you to be confident in the answers that you select.

⊘ KEEP MOVING

Panicking will not help you pass the test, so do your best to stay calm and keep moving. Taking deep breaths and going through the answer elimination steps you practiced can help to break through a stress barrier and keep your pace.

Final Notes

The combination of a solid foundation of content knowledge and the confidence that comes from practicing your plan for applying that knowledge is the key to maximizing your performance on test day. As your foundation of content knowledge is built up and strengthened, you'll find that the strategies included in this chapter become more and more effective in helping you quickly sift through the distractions and traps of the test to isolate the correct answer.

Now that you're preparing to move forward into the test content chapters of this book, be sure to keep your goal in mind. As you read, think about how you will be able to apply this information on the test. If you've already seen sample questions for the test and you have an idea of the question format and style, try to come up with questions of your own that you can answer based on what you're reading. This will give you valuable practice applying your knowledge in the same ways you can expect to on test day.

Good luck and good studying!

Registration of Persons

PERSON

The Uniform Securities Act defines the term person as follows:

"Person" means an individual; corporation; business trust; estate; trust; partnership; limited liability company; association; joint venture; government; governmental subdivision, agency, or instrumentality; public corporation; or any other legal or commercial entity.

Although in general conversation the word person is normally used to describe an individual human being, this word has a different meaning in the Uniform Securities Act. In this context, the term person does not necessarily mean a human being. According to the USA, a person may be an individual human being, but a person may also be a legal entity such as a corporation. An individual is not considered a person in this context if the person is dead, mentally unfit, or a minor.

NATURAL PERSON AND LEGAL PERSON

The term natural person refers to an individual human being. This term is used to refer to an individual that a layperson would call a person in normal conversation (as opposed to legal language). The term legal person refers to an entity that can enter into a contract and have accounts (investments, savings, etc.). Examples of a legal person include a living human being of legal age, a corporation, a partnership, or an estate. When the term person is used in connection with the Uniform Securities Act, the term should be interpreted as a legal person. The term person should not be interpreted to mean natural person unless the term natural person is specifically used.

LEGAL PERSON OR LEGAL ENTITY

A legal person may be an individual or an entity such as a legal partnership, an estate, or a corporation. Whether a legal person is an individual or an entity, all legal persons have a number of characteristics in common. These include:

- Legal persons can enter into contracts with other legal persons.
- Legal persons may engage in business transactions.
- Legal persons, whether an individual or an entity, can be charged with and found guilty of criminal activity.
- Legal persons can be sued and may face civil litigation.
- Legal persons may be required to pay damages if found to be at fault in a civil suit.
- In some instances, both an entity and an individual associated with that entity could be found guilty of the same or associated crimes.

19

REGULATED ENTITIES

The Uniform Securities Act regulates many aspects of the securities industry. The Uniform Securities Act specifically regulates the manner in which the following entities may operate: broker-dealers, investment advisers, agents, and investment adviser representatives. For example, the Uniform Securities Act includes a number of registration requirements that apply specifically to broker-dealers, investment advisers, agents, and investment adviser representatives. The registration process helps to ensure that only qualified parties are licensed to operate; it also provides a means to ensure that these parties' performance meets, and continues to meet, the required standards. The Uniform Securities Act also includes laws that apply broadly to any person. These broad laws are generally designed to address and prevent securities fraud and apply to registered and unregistered parties alike.

PERSONS REQUIRED TO BE REGISTERED

The Uniform Securities Act requires that any person that wishes acts as a broker-dealer, agent, investment adviser, or investment adviser representative must first be registered with the Administrator. It should be noted that the term *person* in this context means legal person. Broker-dealers and investment advisers may be individuals or companies. Agents and investment adviser representatives are always individuals. Any person acting in any of these four capacities must have first applied for, obtained, and maintained registration. The Uniform Securities Act regulates persons acting in any of these four capacities, and the state Administrator oversees their activities. The registration requirement helps to ensure that only qualified persons are able to act in these capacities.

Regulation of Investment Advisers

INVESTMENT ADVISER

An investment adviser is an individual or a company that receives compensation to provide advice to others concerning the investment, purchase, or sale of securities. The advice may be provided directly or indirectly. An example of advice provided directly to a client would be a personal consultation conducted in person or over the phone for a fee. Advice contained in monthly reports that analyzed securities and offered investment advice for a subscription fee would be considered indirect advice. Investment advisers may receive flat fees or fees based on a percentage of managed assets. All persons that are considered investment advisers are regulated and must be registered with the Administrator. The Administrator is responsible for ensuring that investment advisers are qualified to offer the services that they provide.

The Uniform Securities Act defines the term investment adviser as follows:

> "Investment adviser" means a person that, for compensation, engages in the business of advising others, either directly or through publications or writings, as to the value of securities or the advisability of investing in, purchasing, or selling securities or that, for compensation and as a part of a regular business, issues or promulgates analyses or reports concerning securities. The term includes a financial planner or other person that, as an integral component of other financially related services, provides investment advice to others for compensation as part of a business or that holds itself out as providing investment advice to others for compensation.

Please note: the definition contained in the Uniform Securities Act goes on to provide a list of persons that are *not* considered investment advisers.

CHARACTERISTICS

In order to be classified as an investment adviser under the Uniform Securities Act, a person must satisfy three specific requirements. First, the person must offer advice to others concerning securities. The advice provided may be in the form of recommendations regarding the purchase and/or sale of securities, or it may be in the form of an evaluation of the value (immediate, short-term, or long-term) of specific securities. Second, the offering of such advice must be part of the person's continuing line of business. For example, an individual who simply provides an opinion on an investment opportunity during a conversation with an acquaintance may be providing investment advice to the acquaintance, but he or she is not offering that investment advice as part of a line of business. Finally, the person offering the advice must receive compensation for the investment advice that he or she provided.

21

PERSONS NOT CONSIDERED INVESTMENT ADVISERS

Investment adviser representatives are not investment advisers. Investment advisers do not include persons in certain professions that provide purely incidental investment advice as part of their job. For example, an accountant who advised a client to invest funds in a particular manner in order to obtain tax benefits would not be considered an investment adviser. Similarly, a broker-dealer that provided incidental investment advice while acting as a broker-dealer would not be considered an investor adviser if the broker-dealer did not receive compensation for the advice. The publisher of a publication such as a magazine, newspaper, or journal offered through general public circulation is not an investor adviser. Banks and savings institutions and persons whose investment advice only concerns securities offered by the US government and/or specific municipal securities are not investment advisers. Please note that although this discussion illustrates common examples, it is not intended to be all-inclusive.

The definition of investment adviser in the Uniform Securities Act states the term investment adviser does not include:

- An investment adviser representative
- A lawyer, accountant, engineer, or teacher whose performance of investment advice is solely incidental to the practice of the person's profession
- A broker-dealer or its agents whose performance of investment advice is solely incidental to the conduct of business as a broker-dealer and that does not receive special compensation for the investment advice
- A publisher of a bona fide newspaper, news magazine, or business or financial publication of general and regular circulation
- A federal covered investment adviser
- A bank or savings institution
- Any other person that is excluded by the Investment Advisers Act of 1940 from the definition of investment adviser
- Any other person excluded by rule adopted or order issued under this [Act]

PROFESSIONS THAT MAY PROVIDE INVESTMENT ADVICE WITHOUT BEING REGISTERED

The Uniform Securities Act recognizes that individuals in certain professions will need to provide incidental investment advice as part of their day-to-day job duties. The Uniform Securities Act identifies four such professions for which individuals may provide such incidental investment advice without being considered an investment adviser. These four professions are teacher, attorney, engineer, and accountant. Individuals in each of these four professions are exempted from investment adviser registration requirements as long as the investment advice they provide is merely incidental to their primary job functions and the individual does not receive special compensation for providing the investment advice. The key to this exemption is that the investment advice provided by these individuals must be merely an incidental component of the services or instruction otherwise provided.

STATE FILING OBLIGATIONS

The National Securities Markets Improvements Act of 1996 (NSMIA) exempts persons that must register as investment advisers with the Securities Exchange Commission (SEC) from the requirement to register as investment advisers with any state Administrators. However, it is important to note that the NSMIA does not completely eliminate the relationship between a federally covered investment adviser and the state Administrator for the states in which the federally covered investment adviser operates. Although a federally covered investment adviser is not required to register with the state Administrator, each federally covered investment adviser must provide notice of its status to the Administrator and submit payment for the state's required filing fees. The process of providing such notice is referred to as a notice filing. It should be noted that investment adviser representatives for federally covered investment advisers are still required to register with the Administrator.

CONDUCTING BUSINESS IN A STATE WITHOUT BEING REGISTERED

Investment advisers must generally be registered with either the SEC or with each state in which they conduct business; however, there is an exception in some instances when the investment adviser does not have a place of business within the state and is registered in another state. The exception is dependent upon the number and type of clients the investment adviser serves in the state. If the investment adviser's only clients within the state are all registered broker-dealers, investment advisers, institutional investors, and/or persons whose primary residence is an another state where the investment adviser is registered, the investment adviser is not required to register in that state. In addition, if the investment adviser has no more than five clients within the state beyond the type of clients described above, and if the investment adviser is registered in another state, the investment adviser is not obligated to register in the state to conduct business.

BOND REQUIREMENTS

The state Administrator may establish minimum financial standards for investment advisers that operate in the state. If the Administrator requires the investment adviser to post bonds or provide some other form of security, the maximum amount the Administrator may require is limited to the maximum amount permitted under federal regulations. The amount of the bond required is generally dependent upon the amount of authority the investment adviser will have over its clients' funds. If a client grants discretionary authority to an investment adviser to manage the client's accounts, a bond of $10,000 is normally required. If the investment adviser will maintain actual custody of its clients' accounts, a larger bond will normally be required. The standard amount in this case is $35,000.

FIDUCIARY RESPONSIBILITY

The regulations that apply to the prohibited actions for persons engaged in securities transactions are determined by the nature of the activity, not the person's registration status. Regulations that apply to investment advice apply whether the advice is provided by an actual investment adviser or by an agent providing advice in connection with the sale of a security. The highest standards apply to persons acting as investment advisers. Persons that provide investment advice are considered fiduciaries. A fiduciary must put the interests of their clients above their own interests. Persons offering investment advice must meet this standard because they are acting in a position of trust in a capacity that impacts the clients' finances. As part of this requirement, it is imperative that persons offering investment advice inform clients of any potential conflict of interest. These requirements help to ensure that investors can trust the advice provided by their advisers.

ADVERTISING LIMITATIONS

The Uniform Securities Act includes specific limitations regarding the permissible contents of advertisements for investment advisers. Advertisements are classified as a message about the investment adviser that is directed to more than one person. Investment adviser advertisements may not include testimonials of any kind. If the advertisement contains any information regarding the historical performance of the securities recommended by the investment adviser, the advertisement may not limit the information to successful recommendations. Instead, if the advertisement references the performance of a particular recommended stock, the advertisement must reference the performance of all of the recommendations the investment adviser made regarding the same type of securities over that previous year (or longer). If historical performance is referenced, the advertisement must accurately reflect recommendations resulting in losses as well as those resulting in gains.

All these limitations apply to advertising regardless of medium, hence applying equally to physical correspondence, email, social media, and so forth.

Regulation of Investment Adviser Representatives

INVESTMENT ADVICE

An investment adviser must offer advice to its clients regarding securities transactions. However, it is possible for a person or firm to provide investment advice to clients without acting as an investment adviser. An individual or firm is not acting as an investment adviser if the investment advice the individual or firm provides does not concern securities. For example, if an individual or firm provides financial advice to a client regarding investing in federally insured certificates of deposit (CDs), the individual or firm would not be providing advice concerning a securities transaction; therefore, the individual or firm would not be acting as an investment adviser. An individual or firm only acts in the capacity of an investment adviser if the investment advice provided concerns investment in securities.

AGENT AND INVESTMENT ADVISER REPRESENTATIVE

An agent is an individual who is not a broker-dealer, but who acts as a representative of a broker-dealer to handle security purchases and/or security sales. An agent can also be a representative for an issuer of a security who handles the purchase or sale of that issuer's securities. An investment adviser representative is an individual who is not an investment adviser, but who acts as a representative of an investment adviser. Investment adviser representatives include individuals who provide advice regarding securities, handle client accounts and/or portfolios, and/or receive compensation for seeking or obtaining clients for an investment adviser. Investment advisers also include individuals who supervise employees that perform the activities discussed above. Clerical personnel in an investment adviser firm are not considered investment adviser representatives. Agents are sometimes called registered representatives or sales representatives.

The Uniform Securities Act defines the term investment adviser representative as follows:

> "Investment adviser representative" means an individual employed by or associated with an investment adviser or federal covered investment adviser and who makes any recommendations or otherwise gives investment advice regarding securities, manages accounts or portfolios of clients, determines which recommendation or advice regarding securities should be given, provides investment advice or holds herself or himself out as providing investment advice, receives compensation to solicit, offer, or negotiate for the sale of or for selling investment advice, or supervises employees who perform any of the foregoing.

Please note: the definition contained in the Uniform Securities Act goes on to provide a list of persons that are *not* considered investment adviser representatives.

PERSONS NOT CONSIDERED INVESTMENT ADVISER REPRESENTATIVES

Per the Uniform Securities Act, an investment adviser representative is not an individual who:

1. Performs only clerical or ministerial acts;
2. Is an agent whose performance of investment advice is solely incidental to the individual acting as an agent and who does not receive special compensation for investment advisory services;
3. Is employed by or associated with a federal covered investment adviser, unless the individual has a "place of business" in this State as that term is defined by rule adopted under Section 203A of the Investment Advisers Act of 1940 (15 USC. Section 80b-3a) and is (i) an "investment adviser representative" as that term is defined by rule adopted under Section 203A of the Investment Advisers Act of 1940 (15 USC. Section 80b-3a); or (ii) not a "supervised person" as that term is defined in Section 202(a)(25) of the Investment Advisers Act of 1940 (15 USC. Section 80b-2(a)(25); or
4. Is excluded by rule adopted or order issued under this [Act].

REGISTRATION REQUIREMENTS

All investment advisers and investment adviser representatives must be registered. Investment advisers that manage assets of $100 million or more do not register with the state Administrator. Instead, these investment advisers must register with the SEC. Investment advisers that do not manage at least $100 million in assets must register with the state Administrator. Investment advisers must notify the Administrator of each investment adviser representative employed. In certain instances, investment advisers may not be required to be registered in a given state if they are already registered in a different state.

Regulation of Broker-Dealers

BROKER-DEALER

A broker-dealer is an individual or a company (firm) that charges other individuals or entities for handling securities transactions on their behalf. Broker-dealers may receive compensation through fees or commissions. The term broker-dealer does not include agents (representatives of broker-dealers or the issuer of a security); issuers (an entity that makes its own securities available for purchase); international banking institutions; or any other person or entity specifically excluded by the Uniform Security Act. The term broker-dealer does not generally include domestic banks or savings institutions; however, banks and savings institutions may be designated as broker-dealers depending upon the types of activities and transactions it handles. All persons that fall under the definition of broker-dealer must be registered with the Administrator.

The Uniform Securities Act defines the term broker-dealer as follows:

- "'Broker-dealer' means a person engaged in the business of effecting transactions in securities for the account of others or for the person's own account. The term does not include:
  - An agent
  - An issuer
  - A bank or savings institution if its activities as a broker-dealer are limited to those specified in subsections 3(a)(4)(B)(i) through (vi), (viii) through (x), and (xi) if limited to unsolicited transactions; 3(a)(5)(B); and 3(a)(5)(C) of the Securities Exchange Act of 1934 [15 USC. Sections 78c(a)(4) and (5)] or a bank that satisfies the conditions described in subsection 3(a)(4)(E) of the Securities Exchange Act of 1934 [15 USC. Section 78c(a)(4)];
  - An international banking institution
  - A person excluded by rule adopted or order issued under this [Act]"

BROKER ACTIVITIES AND DEALER ACTIVITIES

Any person that is registered as a broker-dealer is authorized to perform in two different capacities. A broker-dealer may perform the functions of a broker and the functions of a dealer. These two activities are distinctly different. A broker-dealer acts as a broker when performing security-trading activities on behalf of its client accounts. For example, if a broker-dealer purchases a security for a client at the client's request, the broker-dealer is acting in the role of a broker. A broker-dealer acts as a dealer when performing trading activities for itself. For example, if a broker-dealer liquidates some of the securities in one of its own accounts, the broker-dealer is acting in the role of a dealer.

REGISTRATION REQUIREMENTS

All broker-dealers and agents must be registered with the Administrator in order to conduct business. Broker-dealers and issuers may only employ agents who have valid registration. The registration for an agent is tied to a specific, registered broker-dealer or a specific issuer, and that registration will remain effective only if the agent remains associated with that specific registered broker-dealer or issuer. For example, if an agent's registration shows that the agent works for "Broker-dealer A," that registration will not be valid if the agent goes to work for "Broker-dealer B." Similarly, an agent's registration will not remain valid if the broker-dealer with whom the agent is associated loses its license for any reason. The Administrator must be notified any time there is a change in an agent's association with a particular broker-dealer. In such instances, both the broker-dealer and the agent must inform the Administrator of the change.

REGISTRATION APPLICATION

Each person desiring to obtain registration as a broker-dealer, investment adviser, agent, or investment adviser representative from a state Administrator in order to conduct business in a given state must first meet all of the requirements for the desired registration. In order to register, the applicant must submit a completed application to the Administrator. The applicant must also render the designated payment amount required for the type of license requested. In addition to the application and associated fees, the applicant must post any bonds that have been required by the state Administrator. If the Administrator requires an examination for registration, the applicant must complete all of the required examination successfully. If examinations are required, the format may be oral and/or written. Finally, the applicant must provide consent to service of process to the Administrator.

ADDITIONAL APPLICATION REQUIREMENTS

During the initial registration process, applying broker-dealers, investment advisers, agents, and investment adviser representatives must include a consent to service of process with the application. In the event the applicant becomes involved in a civil suit from within or outside the state, the consent to service of process allows the litigating party to serve papers for the applicant by simply serving them on the Administrator. It may also be necessary to meet financial qualifications. Broker-dealers and investment advisers may be required to meet minimum requirements for net capital. In addition, the Administrator may require broker-dealers, investment advisers, agents, and investment adviser representatives to obtain and maintain surety bonds up to $10,000. If required, the deposit for the surety bonds may be made by cash or securities. If securities are used to secure the surety bond, the Administrator may specify the type of security that may be used.

REQUIREMENTS TO RETAIN LICENSING AFTER REGISTRATION

The state Administrator may require both broker-dealers and investment advisers to file various financial reports. All of the information contained in documents filed with the Administrator must not only be accurate and complete at the time of filing, the documents must also remain accurate and complete after filing. If changes occur after the information has been filed with the Administrator, and any of information contained in a field document is no longer accurate or complete, the filing party must correct the document by filing an amendment. Licenses are valid for no longer than a year. The renewal process requires that the registrant pay a fee. If the registrant does not renew prior to the license's expiration, the license will expire at the end of the year (on December 31).

DUAL REGISTRATION

Persons that are registered as broker-dealers may also be registered as investment advisers. A person that wishes to be registered as a broker-dealer and as an investment adviser must submit applications and accompanying fees for both. In order to obtain licenses in both capacities, the applicant person must meet all of the requirements established by the Administrator for both licenses. If the Administrator determines that a party that is seeking to register as a broker-dealer and an investment adviser is not qualified to act as an investment adviser, the Administrator may order that the broker-dealer's license be established *only* on the condition that the party refrains from operating as an investment adviser. In this instance, the requesting party's broker-dealer license would be invalidated if the party acted as an investor adviser.

REGISTRATION FOR SUCCESSORS

Registration for broker-dealers and investment advisers may be transferred if the broker-dealer or investment adviser has a successor. In the event a firm that is currently registered as a broker-dealer and/or as an investment adviser has, or will have, a successor during any given year, that firm may submit an application for the registration of that successor firm. If a registered firm knows that it will have a successor during the year, it may submit the application on behalf of that successor before the successor firm ever comes into existence. When a currently registered firm registers a successor firm in this manner, the successor firm will be allowed to operate under the previous firm's registration for the rest of the year. No additional registration fee is required when registering a successor firm.

AUTOMATIC REGISTRATION

The registration of a broker-dealer or an investment adviser may cause the automatic registration of individuals associated with the broker-dealer or investment adviser. When a broker-dealer is registered, all of the directors, partners and/or officers for the broker-dealer, as well as any individual acting in a similar capacity, that are active participants in the broker-dealer's registered activities will automatically be registered as agents. Along the same lines, when an investment adviser registers with the Administrator, all of the directors, partners and/or officers for the investment adviser, as well as any individual acting in a similar capacity, who are active participants in the investment adviser's registered activities will automatically be registered as investment adviser representatives. Although the registration is automatic in these instances, the Administrator may require examinations.

PROVISIONS GOVERNING CLIENTS TEMPORARILY IN OTHER STATES

If a broker-dealer or investment adviser is registered in one state, it may conduct business with its clients that are residents of that state even when those clients are traveling outside of the state. This provision of the Uniform Securities Act enables broker-dealers and investment advisers to provide continual service to their client base while their clients travel outside of their home state. Without this provision, broker-dealers and investment advisers would have to be registered in every state their clients may visit. In addition, in instances where a broker-dealer or investment adviser's existing client relocates to a state in which the broker-dealer or investment adviser is not registered, the broker-dealer or investment adviser may continue to serve this existing client for thirty days.

EXCLUSIONS ALLOWING A LEGAL PERSON TO NOT REGISTER WITH A STATE AS A BROKER-DEALER

Not all legal persons that perform securities transactions for themselves and others fall under the definition of broker-dealer. Specifically excluded from the definition of broker-dealer are agents who transact of behalf of others, issuers of securities, banks, savings and loan institutions, and trust companies. Some broker-dealers qualify for exemption from registration in certain states. If a broker-dealer has no place of business within a given state and only transacts with other financial institutions within the state, it is excluded from the registration requirement for that given state. Additionally, if a broker-dealer is registered in a state in which it conducts business, only offers to sell securities within that state, and a non-resident person purchases those securities within the same state, the broker-dealer is excluded from registration in the purchaser's state.

INVESTMENT ADVISER REPRESENTATIVE

An investment adviser representative is an employee, or representative, of a registered investment adviser. On behalf of the registered investment advisor, they may (or may not) make recommendations regarding securities, manage client funds, offer investment advisory services (e.g., wrap fee accounts), or supervise employees who do any or all of the above. Investment adviser representatives are not registered investment advisers, and may not offer advisory services on their own behalf; rather, they may solicit advisory services on behalf of a registered investment advisor. Investment adviser representatives act on behalf of the registered firm. It is important to distinguish between the two terms, since they are easily confused. Registered investment advisers are often abbreviated as RIAs, whereas investment advisor representatives are abbreviated as IARs; this fact can often worsen the confusion.

Regulation of Agents of Broker-Dealers

AGENT

The Uniform Securities Act defines the term agent as follows:

> "Agent" means an individual, other than a broker-dealer, who represents a broker-dealer in effecting or attempting to effect purchases or sales of securities or represents an issuer in effecting or attempting to effect purchases or sales of the issuer's securities. But a partner, officer, or director of a broker-dealer or issuer, or an individual having a similar status or performing similar functions is an agent only if the individual otherwise comes within the term. The term does not include an individual excluded by rule adopted or order issued under this [Act].

EXCEPTIONS TO REQUIREMENT THAT BROKER-DEALERS BE REGISTERED IN THE STATE THEY DO BUSINESS

For the most part, broker-dealers must be registered as broker-dealers in each state in which they conduct business. However, there are exceptions to this requirement. If the person has a business location within the state, the person must register with that state's Administrator. However, if the person does not have any business location within the state, the person may conduct business without registering with the Administrator as long as the person only engages in transactions through or for financial institutions, issuers, and/or other broker dealers. In addition, a broker-dealer that is registered in one state may conduct transactions outside of that state on behalf of current clients that have primary residence in the state in which the broker-dealer is registered while those clients travel to a state in which the broker-dealer is not registered.

REPRESENTING MULTIPLE PERSONS

As a general rule, registered agents may only represent a single registered broker-dealer or a single registered issuer; however, this is not always the case. A registered agent may represent multiple registered broker-dealers or multiple registered issuers if all of the broker-dealers or issuers are affiliated with each other. For purposes of this rule, to be considered affiliated, each of the broker-dealers or issuers must have a shared controller. If the broker-dealers or issuers in question are not affiliated in this manner, an agent may still be permitted to represent them if the Administrator gives authorization for the agent to operate under multiple licenses. Unless these circumstances occur, the agent may only represent a single broker-dealer or issuer.

TERMINATING REGISTRATION

Registered persons may not simply abandon their employment to terminate their responsibilities. In the event that registered individuals decide of their own volition to terminate their registration, their employing agency must notify the Financial Industry Regulatory Authority (FINRA) in writing at least 30 days prior to that individual's termination. If the situation is one such as retirement, that individual may enter a contract with his or her employing firm to continue receiving commissions for which they were responsible for generating. In the event that a FINRA member firm decides to terminate a registrant's registration and that person is under investigation by FINRA or another self-regulatory organization, that firm must wait until the investigations conclude before terminating the registration.

PROCESS FOR CLIENTS WITH MARGIN ACCOUNTS

A broker-dealer must follow special procedures when dealing with clients that possess margin accounts. In addition to the standard requirement that the broker-dealer has to obtain client authorization prior to engaging in a securities transaction, a broker-dealer with a margin account must obtain an effective written margin agreement from its client. Although the broker-dealer must obtain standard client authorization prior to initiating any transaction in the client's margin account, the broker-dealer may initiate the first transaction in the client's margin account before the broker-dealer possesses an effective written margin agreement. If the broker-dealer has not obtained a valid, executed margin agreement from the client prior to the initial margin account transaction, the broker-dealer must obtain such agreement shortly after the initial transaction. Failure to obtain a margin agreement from the client in a timely manner may be grounds for the Administrator to deny, suspend, or revoke the broker-dealer's registration.

BROKER-DEALER'S OBLIGATION TO MAKE ONLY LEGITIMATE OFFERS

Each and every offer a broker-dealer makes to buy or sell a security must be a legitimate offer. Broker-dealers must only make offers to buy a security from a client, or to sell a security to a client, if the broker-dealer is truly prepared to follow through with the offer at the specified terms if accepted. For example, assume that a broker-dealer is aware that a particular client has limited funds to invest at the moment. It would be unethical for that broker-dealer to make an offer to sell securities to the client at a low price simply because the broker-dealer knew that the client did not have the funds needed to accept the offer. It is unscrupulous for a broker-dealer to make any offer to buy or sell securities unless the broker-dealer is truly ready, willing, and able to honor the terms of the offer.

Regulations of Securities and Issuers

SECURITY

The Uniform Securities Act defines *security* as "a note; stock; treasury stock; security future; bond; debenture; evidence of indebtedness; certificate of interest or participation in a profit-sharing agreement; collateral trust certificate; pre-organization certificate or subscription; transferable share; investment contract; voting trust certificate; certificate of deposit for a security; fractional undivided interest in oil, gas, or other mineral rights; put, call, straddle, option, or privilege on a security, certificate of deposit, or group or index of securities, including an interest therein or based on the value thereof; put, call, straddle, option, or privilege entered into on a national securities exchange relating to foreign currency; or, in general, an interest or instrument commonly known as a 'security'; or a certificate of interest or participation in, temporary or interim certificate for, receipt for, guarantee of, or warrant or right to subscribe to or purchase, any of the foregoing."

TYPES OF SECURITIES AVAILABLE TO BE SOLD

The Uniform Securities Act specifies that securities are only eligible to be sold (or offered for sale) if the security falls into one of three categories. In order to be lawfully available for sale within the state, a security must either be a federally covered security, a security that is currently registered with the state Administrator in accordance with the provisions of the Uniform Securities Act, or a security that is exempt from both federal and state registration. It is illegal for any person to sell or offer to sell any security that does not fall under one of the categories listed above. This requirement applies whether the person selling, or offering to sell, the security as a registered securities professional (such as a broker-dealer) or not.

INVESTMENT CONTRACTS

Investment contracts are considered securities. One form of an investment contract is a financial investment in a common enterprise in which the investor hopes to receive profits as a result of the work of others. A common enterprise exists when the profits and losses of the investor are tied to the profits and losses of (a) other investors, (b) the party offering the investment, or (c) a third party. One example of such an investment contract is an investment providing a 5% ownership interest in a chicken farm. If the farm were profitable, the investor with a 5% ownership interest would realize a profit. If the farm were to suffer a loss, the investor would suffer a loss as well. Another example of an investment contract is an investment providing interest in a limited partnership. These investments are considered securities.

REGISTRATION BY COORDINATION

Issuers that intend to register a security with the SEC that must also be registered with state Administrators may use the process of registration by coordination. The registration by coordination process is designed to minimize the unnecessary duplication of effort between state and federal securities regulators. The process is

33

typically used in cases when a security must be registered with the SEC because it is an interstate offering (an offering that will be made available in more than one state) but the issuer is not large enough to be exempted from state registration. Under the registration by coordination process, each of the state registrations will become effective at the same time as or after the SEC registration becomes effective.

NOTIFICATION PROCEDURES

Issuers seeking to register a security with a state Administrator under the registration by coordination process are required to follow specific notification procedures. The issuer must provide timely notification to the state Administrator of the date that the federal registration of the security becomes effective. Issuers must also provide prompt notification to the Administrator if there are any changes to the pricing amendment and if so, explain the nature of the change and file a copy of the modified pricing amendment. If the issuer does not provide this notice promptly, the Administrator may issue a stop order without prior notice or hearing. The Administrator may also issue a retroactive denial of the security's registration or suspend registration pending the receipt of the required notice and documentation.

DOCUMENTATION REQUIREMENTS

In addition to the standard registration statement and consent to service of process, issuers requesting state registration under the registration by coordination process must provide the Administrator with copies of: the most recent form of the prospectus filed with the SEC under the provisions of the Securities Act of 1933; the articles of incorporation and current bylaws (or equivalent); any agreement that exists between or with the underwriters; and any indenture or instrument that governs the issuance of the security. The issuer must also provide a copy, sample, or description of the security. The issuer must also update the filing by forwarding any amendments, other than amendments that postpone the effective date of the federal registration, to the federal prospectus in a timely manner. In addition, the state Administrator may also require that the issuer file copies of additional information.

EFFECTIVE DATE FOR REGISTRATION

The effective date for securities registered under the registration by coordination process is tied to the effective date of the federal registration; a security's registration in a given state cannot become effective prior to the federal registration. The state-level registration will become effective when the federal registration is effective if the SEC has not issued a stop order or started a proceeding to suspend, deny, or revoke registration, and if the registration statement has been on file with the state Administrator for twenty days (or a shorter period designated by the Administrator). If the previous conditions are not met at the time the federal registration becomes effective, the state registration will become effective when these conditions are met. For example, if the registration statement has been on file with the state Administrator for ten days when the federal registration becomes effective, the state registration will become effective ten days later.

REGISTRATION BY QUALIFICATION

Registration by qualification is the most difficult method of registering a security with a state Administrator. Registration by qualification is the process that must be followed if the security in question must be registered with the state Administrator, but the security (or issuer) does not qualify for registration under either the registration by coordination process or the registration by filing (also known as the registration by notification process). Issuers seeking to register a security by qualification must provide a significant amount of detailed information with the registration statement in addition to the standard filing requirements for securities (including the consent to service of process). The registration of securities registered under the registration by qualification process does not become effective automatically. The registration only becomes effective if and when ordered by the Administrator.

INFORMATION REGARDING A SECURITY

When an issuer seeks to obtain registration for a security under the registration by qualification process, the issuer must provide a detailed description of the security offering as well as the sales-related materials the issuer intends to use. The description of the security itself must include either an actual representative sample of the security itself or a copy of the security. The issuer must also include a signed statement from an attorney that attests that the planned offering of the security the issuer seeks to register is legal. In addition to the security itself, the issuer must provide copies of any promotional material (e.g., pamphlets, advertisements, letters, prospectus, flyers, etc.) that will be used in connection with the offer.

INFORMATION REGARDING THE ISSUER'S DIRECTORS AND OFFICERS

When the issuer registers a security using the registration by qualification process, the registration statement for the security must include specific information regarding the issuer's officers and directors. The registration statement must provide the name and address of each and every one of the issuer's directors and officers and indicate the primary employment for the preceding five years for each of the issuer's directors and officers. In addition to this biographical information, the issuer must specify the volume of the issuer's securities possessed by each officer and director as of a date that is no earlier than thirty days prior to the date of filing, and the issue must also specify the volume of the security or securities to be registered that each director and officer plans to possess. Finally, the issuer must state the actual compensation for each director and officer for the previous year and the anticipated compensation for the next year.

INFORMATION REGARDING THE ISSUER

The application for registration for securities registered by qualification must include a significant amount of information regarding the issuer of the security. In addition to the issuer's name and address, the registration must contain information regarding the facts surrounding the issuer's business organization. The required information includes the state (or foreign country, if applicable) that has jurisdiction over the issuer's company organization; the structure of the issuer's organization (*e.g.*, corporation, limited partnerships, etc.); and the date of the issuer's organization. The registration statement must also list any equipment and material property owned by the issuer. Finally, the registration statement must include a discussion of the competitive environment for the type of business in which the issuer operates (or will operate).

INFORMATION REGARDING THE SECURITY OFFERING

Issuers that register a security with the state Administrator using the registration by qualification process must provide a detailed account of the offering, including the type of security to be offered, the anticipated offer price for the securities, and the volume of securities to be offered. The registration statement must also estimate the compensation that will be given to the underwriters and the amount of any anticipated finder's fees. If a party other than the issuer will sell any of the securities covered by the registration statement, the issuer must explain why another party or parties will be selling the security, identify each distributor, and identify the quantity of the security allotted to each distributor at the time of the filing.

INFORMATION REGARDING THE ISSUER'S LARGE INVESTORS

In addition to information regarding the issuer's officers and directors, an issuer seeking to register a security by qualification must also provide information concerning any individual that owns ten percent (or more) of the issuer's securities. For each individual, other than the issuer's officers and directors, that owns ten percent or more of the issuer's securities, the issuer must specify the volume of securities held by the individual as of a date that is no later than thirty days prior to date the security registration statement is filed. In addition, for the security (or securities) that are the subject of the registration request, the issuer must indicate the volume that each such individual intends to possess upon approval of registration.

INFORMATION REGARDING THE PLANNED ISSUANCE OF THE SECURITY

Issuers seeking to register a security under the registration by qualification process must include a discussion regarding the plans associated with the issuance of the security. To begin with, this discussion must identify any stock options associated with the security offering that have been granted or that will be granted. The discussion of any stock options must note the volumes to be possessed by each of the issuer's officers and directors as well as each individual that owns ten percent or more of the issuer's securities. The registration statement must also provide an estimate of the anticipated revenue to be generated by the issuance of the security as well as a breakdown of how that revenue will be used. If the anticipated revenue will be used in an area that is also receives revenue from another source, the statement must also describe the additional source.

FINANCIAL INFORMATION THE ISSUER MUST PROVIDE

Issuers that seek to register securities with a state Administrator under the registration by qualification process must include financial information with the registration statement. The issuer must include a current balance sheet that reflects data that was current no more than four months prior to the filing. Starting from the date used in the calculation of the balance sheet, the issuer must also provide a statement of its income for each of the three previous fiscal years. In the event the issuer intends to use some or all of the proceeds from the sale of the security to finance the purchase of another company or business, the registration statement must also include all of the information listed above for that company or business as well. In addition to the information listed above, the registration statement must note all of the issuer's long-term debt and capitalization.

REGISTRATION BY NOTIFICATION
REQUIRED DOCUMENTATION

Issuers that register a security with the state Administrator using the registration by filing process (also known as the registration by notification process) must submit additional documentation with the security's registration statement. In addition to the standard requirements, the issuer must demonstrate that they are qualified to register by this method. The issuer must also provide a description of their business that notes the business' location, type of operation, and length of operation. The registration statement must also be accompanied by a description of the security to be registered. Finally, if any of the securities will sold by a party other than the issuer, the issuer must explain why another party or parties will be selling the security and identify each distributor and the quantity of the security allotted to each distributor at the time of the filing

ADDITIONAL INFORMATION FROM BUSINESSES OPERATIONAL FOR FEWER THAN FIVE YEARS

Special requirements apply to issuers of securities seeking to register a security using the registration by filing process (also known as the registration by notification process) if the issuer has been in business for less than five continuous years. Issuers falling into this category may still use the registration by filing process, if otherwise qualified. However, such issuers must provide additional information along with the information and documentation normally required for this type of filing. First, issuers that have not been in business continually for five years must provide a summary of their earnings for the two previous fiscal years. In addition, the issuer must provide a balance sheet for the business that covers the four-month period immediately preceding the filing.

EFFECTIVE REGISTRATION DATE

The registration for securities that are registered using the registration by filing process (also known as the registration by notification process) typically become effective shortly after the registration request is filed with the Administrator. Except as noted below, when an issuer files a request to register a security under the registration by filing process, the registration will automatically become effective at 3:00 p.m. Eastern Standard Time on the second business day after the request for registration is filed. The state Administrator may order an earlier effective date. The registration would not become automatically effective if the Administrator had issued a stop order (deny, suspend, or revoke) or if a proceeding regarding the security's registration is currently pending.

37

DENIAL, SUSPENSION, OR REVOCATION OF REGISTRATION

Securities must be registered with the Administrator; however, the Administrator may deny, suspend, revoke, or cancel registration for a security under certain circumstances. With the exception of instances in which a security's registration is incomplete or inaccurate, the circumstances in which a security's registration may not be approved or may be revoked all involve instances in which the party registering the security is engaged in unethical, fraudulent, and/or inappropriate business practices. For example, the registration for a security may be revoked if the Administrator determines that the registrant is charging fees that are unjustifiably high or that the registrant is involved in any fraudulent security offering. This power of the Administrator is separate from the Administrator's power to deny, suspend, or revoke the registration of a broker-dealer, investment adviser, agent, or investment adviser representative. Both of these powers help the Administrator protect investors.

QUALIFICATION ISSUES

The Administrator may choose to deny, suspend, or revoke an applicant's registration if the applicant is not operating in accordance with the requirements of the Uniform Securities Act. The Administrator may take this type of action in instances when the applicant does not meet the minimum required financial standards. Failure in this area may occur prior to the approval of the application, leading to denial of the registration; it may also occur after approval, leading to suspension or revocation of the registration. The Administrator may also take action to deny, suspend, or revoke an applicant's registration if the Administrator finds that the applicant has intentionally violated any of the provisions of the Uniform Securities Act or has engaged in fraudulent or unethical securities practices.

APPLICATION PROBLEMS

The Administrator may deny, suspend, or revoke an applicant's registration if the Administrator determines that there are significant problems with the party's application. To begin with, the application must be complete. If the application does not include all required information, or if the application contains false or misleading information, the Administrator may deny the application or, if the problem is found after the registration has been approved, the Administrator may suspend or revoke the registration. The Administrator may also deny, revoke, or suspend a registration in instances when the Administrator determines that the applicant does not have the knowledge, experience, or training needed to qualify, or if the applicant has not paid the required filing fees.

HISTORICAL CIRCUMSTANCES

An Administrator may deny, suspend, or revoke an applicant's registration based on the applicant's previous history both in and out of the state. If the applicant has been convicted of a securities-related misdemeanor or any felony in any state at any time within the last ten years, the Administrator may deny, suspend, or revoke the applicant's registration. The Administrator may also deny, suspend, or revoke registration if any court in any state has ordered the applicant to refrain from conducting business in the securities industry, or if an Administrator in any other state has denied, suspended, or revoked the applicant's registration. All of these circumstances have been determined to be significant enough to support an Administrator's decision to not allow an applicant to register and operate within a state.

SUBSTANTIVE ISSUES

The Administrator will suspend, revoke or deny the registration of a security if there are significant concerns regarding the offering. For example, registration will not be granted if the current or planned business practices of the security's issuer are illegal. Registration will not be granted if there has been an intentional violation of the Administrator's rules or orders or the provisions of the Uniform Securities Act in association with the offering of the security. The Administrator will also consider any court injunction or Administrator's stop order issued by another state or federal jurisdiction. The Administrator will also consider the terms of the offering. Registration will not be granted if the offering of the security has been or will be fraudulent. Finally, the Administrator will not grant registration if the compensation mechanisms for the underwriters and/or promoters are not consistent with ethical business practices.

PRELIMINARY PROSPECTUS

During the period after registration with the Securities and Exchange Commission (SEC) but before sale of the registered security may begin, broker-dealers are permitted to seek out potential investors for the security. Individuals that have indicated that they may be interested must be sent a preliminary prospectus. The preliminary prospectus contains all of the same information as the prospectus that will be offered once the security is offered for sale except for the offering price and the date the security is available. The preliminary prospectus provides potential investors with the information necessary to analyze the potential investment in advance of the offering so that a quick decision is possible once the offering price is made known. The preliminary prospectus is also referred to as a *red herring* because it is required to contain a notification in the document, in red, that the document is not an attempt to sell the security.

TIMING FOR OFFERING SECURITIES AFTER REGISTRATION WITH THE SEC

Under the provisions of federal law, issuers that register a security with the Securities and Exchange Commission (SEC) may not begin sales for the security immediately following registration. Instead, issuers must wait for a period of at least twenty days before engaging in any sales activity for the recently registered security. During this waiting period, broker-dealers are permitted to canvas their clients to solicit indications of interest. An indication of interest is an indication that the client may be interested in investing in the security once it is available; however, no sales material (literature, cost information, etc.) may be provided to potential investors during the waiting period. Until the time that sales of the security may begin, no actual deals involving the security may be made or planned. Investors cannot be given the opportunity to purchase the security, or be made aware of the offering price of the security, until the date the security becomes available.

SALE AND OFFER OF SALE OF A SECURITY

The Administrator has jurisdiction over the sale of covered securities and other activities related to the sale. A security sale is any transaction in which the ownership of the security is transferred from one party to another party for compensation. The compensation in a security contract for sale may be monetary, but the exchange of money is not a requirement. If a security is transferred for anything of value, the transaction is considered a sale. An offer to sell a security occurs when one party extends an offer to another party to transfer the ownership of a security for compensation of value, whether monetary or otherwise. Regulated securities transactions include instances where a party offers a security as an incentive or bonus offering to encourage the sale of a non-security.

ASSESSABLE STOCKS

An assessable stock is a stock offered below value in exchange for an assumption of liability. The owner of an assessable stock is liable for the price difference between the offered price and the true value of the stock. Because the transfer of an assessable stock involves the transfer of the stock's associated liability, the transfer of assessable stock is a regulated transaction even if the stock is transferred as a gift. Such transactions fall under the jurisdiction of the Administrator. Assessable stocks no longer exist. Gifts involving non-assessable stocks are handled differently. Gifts of non-assessable stocks are not considered regulated transactions and do not require the oversight of the Administrator.

FEDERALLY COVERED SECURITIES

Federally covered securities are securities that are governed by federal laws and overseen by federal regulators instead of by the Uniform Securities Act and state Administrators. The New York Stock Exchange (NYSE), the NASDAQ National Market, and the NYSE MKT LLC (formerly NYSE Amex) list nationally traded securities. (NASDAQ-traded securities other than those on the National Market are subject to state regulation.) The federal-level Securities and Exchange Commission (SEC) regulates the nationally traded securities. States are prohibited from regulating federally covered securities and transactions. The prohibition against state regulation includes prohibitions against any state-required registration of entities or securities that are covered by federal securities regulation. Securities offered by the federal government are always considered federally covered securities. Securities that are offered by state and local governments are federally covered if the security is offered nationally or outside the state in which security's issuer (the state or local government) is located.

DETERMINATION OF ADMINISTRATOR'S JURISDICTION

A state Administrator's jurisdiction over a particular transaction is determined, in part, by the location in which various activities associated with the transaction have occurred. Multiple state Administrators may have jurisdiction over a particular transaction. Jurisdiction is determined by the state in which the offer to sell the security originated, the state in which any offer to sell the security was directed (for example, the state to which an offer was sent to a potential client through the mail), and the state in which an offer to sell the security is accepted. In instances where an offer is originated in one state, is directed to another state, and is accepted in yet another state, three different state Administrators would have jurisdiction over the transaction.

ORIGINS OF EARLY FEDERAL SECURITIES REGULATIONS

State laws governing securities transactions were enacted well before any federal securities legislation became effective. By the time the Great Depression began in 1929, all of the states had adopted some form of legislation that regulated securities transactions; however, no federal laws governing securities had been implemented. The stock market crash of 1929 changed this In response to the crisis, after the stock market crash, the United States government developed the first national securities regulations. Early directives adopted by the federal government included the Securities Act of 1933 and the Securities Exchange Act of 1934. Since that time, both federal and state governments have remained involved in the regulation of securities.

DEVELOPMENT OF EARLY STATE-SPECIFIC SECURITIES REGULATIONS

The development of state laws concerning securities followed the development of industry in the United States. The growth of industry spawned the development of the supporting financial markets. In the United States, corporations have historically offered securities as a means of raising funds. Corporations made offerings of securities available to the public in order to raise the capital necessary to back expansion and innovation. As this practice became prevalent across the country, states began to adopt laws regulating securities transactions. While this practice was often beneficial for both the offering corporation and the public investors, unethical parties began using securities transactions to trick others into paying money for virtually worthless securities. Individual states responded by drafting laws addressing securities transactions. These state laws were designed to protect investors from fraudulent and/or unethical securities schemes.

UNIFORM SECURITIES ACT

The Uniform Securities Act (USA) is model legislation that was drafted through collaboration involving regulators, attorneys, and industry participants. The purpose of the USA is to provide model legislation that may be adopted in multiple states in an effort to establish uniform, understandable laws across the states. The first Uniform Securities Act was established in 1930; the second Uniform Securities Act replaced it in 1956. The Uniform Securities Act of 1956 was widely adopted. The 1956 Act was revised in 1985, and further amendments were made in 1988. The fourth Uniform Securities Act, approved in 2002, reflects four years of industry collaboration. The 2002 Uniform Securities Act replaces the 1956 and 1985 Acts. As model legislation, the Uniform Securities Act is designed to serve as a baseline for actual legislation within a given jurisdiction.

APPLICABILITY

The Uniform Securities Act provides specific criteria that establish the parties that are subject to regulation by a state Administrator under the Act. The Uniform Securities Act governs securities transactions as well as many of the various individuals and firms involved in conducting securities transactions or providing security-related investment advice. The Uniform Securities Act specifically defines the characteristics of the individuals and entities that are subject to regulation under the Act. The Uniform Securities Act is applicable in any jurisdiction where it has been adopted as legislation. The Uniform Securities Act was developed as a means to provide consistent regulation across a number of states and was designed to protect investors and promote the public interests.

GENERAL ENFORCEMENT PROVISIONS

The Uniform Securities Act includes provisions designed to support the enforcement of the various requirements of the Act. The Uniform Securities Act states that violations of the act may result in civil liabilities and/or criminal penalties. Civil liabilities are financial in nature. The Uniform Securities Act provides that investors may recover funds lost through investments due to the fraudulent or prohibited activities of another party. In addition, an injured investor may be granted compensation for the investor's attorney fees. Persons engaging in fraudulent activities as defined by the Uniform Securities Act may also face criminal charges. In some instances, violators will be charged with criminal violations in addition to being required to pay for civil liabilities. These enforcement provisions are designed to promote compliance and to protect the public interest.

INTERACTION WITH FEDERAL RULES AND REGULATIONS

In addition to knowing the provisions of the Uniform Securities Act, it is important to know the federal laws and regulations that interact with or complement the provisions of the Uniform Securities Act. The Series 63 Exam covers the provisions of the Uniform Securities Act. In many cases, the provisions of the Uniform Securities Act reference federal laws and regulations. As a result, it is important to be somewhat familiar with the federal laws and regulations applying to securities and securities transactions. These laws establish the requirements associated with the registration of certain securities and persons with the Securities and Exchange Commission (SEC) and establish provisions concerning acceptable business practices for security-related dealings.

SECURITIES ACT OF 1933 AND THE SECURITIES EXCHANGE ACT OF 1934

The Securities Act of 1933 and the Securities Exchange Act of 1934 were enacted after the stock market crash of 1929. These pieces of legislation were designed to create accountability for the issuers of securities and to provide protection to the investing public. Together these acts established the standards requiring that certain securities, persons, exchanges, and associations be registered with the Securities and Exchange Commission (SEC), while others are exempt. These acts require that specific information be provided to the SEC and potential investors. For each security that must be registered, the issuer's registration statement must include all of the information regarding the security that will be disclosed to potential investors in an understandable format. If material information is missing from the disclosure, or if the disclosure information is not readily understandable, the SEC will require the issuer to modify the disclosure information before the registration may become effective.

NATIONAL SECURITIES MARKETS IMPROVEMENTS ACT OF 1996

The National Securities Markets Improvements Act of 1996 is generally referred to by its acronym, NSMIA. The NSMIA established a division of responsibility between state regulators and federal regulators. Under the provisions of the NSMIA, the responsibility for regulating certain investment advisers and securities falls to the Securities and Exchange Commission (SEC). An investment adviser that falls under the jurisdiction of the SEC is referred to as a federal covered adviser and is not subject to investor adviser regulation by the Administrator of the Uniform Securities Act. Federal covered advisers must register with the SEC. The investment advisers and securities that are not regulated by the SEC continue to be regulated by the Administrator under the Uniform Securities Act.

SLUSA

The Securities Litigation Uniform Standards Act of 1998 (SLUSA) is federal legislation that was adopted to provide more equality in regards to class action suits relating to securities transactions. The Securities Litigation Uniform Standards Act of 1998 gives federal courts the ability to assert jurisdiction over class actions suits involving securities fraud that have been filed in any given state and to preempt the state courts. This legislation was enacted to ensure federal courts would evaluate any class-action suit involving securities fraud using uniform federal laws regardless of the state in which the alleged fraud occurred. By requiring that class actions suits involving securities fraud be handled by federal courts in accordance with nationally applicable law, SLUSA helps to ensure that such cases will be handled consistently regardless of location.

OBJECTIVES OF THE UNIFORM SECURITIES ACT VS. THE NSMIA OF 1996

The National Conference of Commissioners on Uniform State Laws (NCCUSL) drafted the Uniform Securities Act. The goal of the Uniform Securities Act was to provide model legislation in an effort to promote the implementation of consistent security regulations across state lines. Congress drafted the National Securities Markets Improvements Act of 1996 (NSMIA). NSMIA was designed to eliminate the conflicts that existed between the many state regulations and the federal regulations, and to generate efficiency by establishing a clear division of responsibilities between the state regulators and the federal regulators. The NSMIA eliminated the duplication of efforts that existed between federal and state governments under previous legislation by defining the specific securities and transactions that would fall under federal jurisdiction.

INVESTMENT COMPANY ACT OF 1940

The Investment Company Act of 1940 is federal legislation that provides the definition of an investment company. The Act requires that all investment companies register with the Securities and Exchange Commission (SEC). Investment companies and investment company securities are federally covered and are not subject to registration with state Administrators. In addition to establishing registration requirements for investment companies, the Investment Company Act of 1940 also outlines the restrictions and duties that apply to investment offerings that investment companies make available to the public. Although investment companies are federally regulated and not subject to registration with state administrators, state administrators do retain the authority to enforce any investment company violations of the anti-fraud provisions of the Uniform Securities Act.

INVESTMENT ADVISERS ACT OF 1940

The Investment Advisers Act of 1940 establishes the provisions governing investment advisers. This legislation dictates which investment advisers must register with the Securities and Exchange Commission (SEC). Investment advisers that are required to register with the SEC are considered federal covered advisers. Investment advisers that are not required to register with the SEC may be required to register with a state Administrator (or state Administrators) unless the investment adviser is exempt from state registration as well. An investment advisory firm may be a federally covered investment adviser (registered with the SEC), and yet, the firm's investment adviser representatives may still need to be registered with the state Administrator. The fact that an investment adviser is federally regulated does not mean that its representatives are federally regulated as well.

SECURITIES INVESTOR PROTECTION ACT OF 1970

The Securities Investor Protection Act of 1970 is federal legislation that established the Securities Investor Protection Corporation (SIPC). The SIPC is a federally mandated insurance company that serves to insure securities investors in the event the investor's broker-dealer defaults for one reason or another. The SIPC protects investors in the event of a broker-dealer bankruptcy as well as in instances of broker-dealer fraud by providing coverage to investors for up to five hundred thousand dollars. Broker-dealers are members of the SIPC and provide the funding for its operation. The SIPC is a non-profit corporation. It should be noted that although the SIPC provides nationwide protection to the clients of broker-dealers, the SIPC is not a federal regulatory body or an agency of the federal government.

TRUST INDENTURE ACT OF 1939 AND THE PUBLIC UTILITY HOLDING COMPANY ACT OF 1935

The Trust Indenture Act of 1939 is federal legislation that applies to large, publicly issued debt securities. The Trust Indenture Act of 1939 establishes special requirements for any publicly issued debt security that exceeds five million dollars within any given twelve-month time frame. Under the provisions of this act, such debt securities may only be issued under a trust indenture. In order to comply with this requirement, the trust indenture must contain specified protections that provide safeguards for the bondholders. The Public Utility Holding Company Act of 1935 is federal legislation requiring that holding companies for gas and electric utilities be federally registered unless specifically exempted from registration. This legislation was designed to guard against abuses by such companies.

SECURITIES INVESTOR PROTECTION CORPORATION VS. FDIC

The FDIC provides guarantees to persons who place deposits in covered banks. The FDIC provides insurance against loss up to a fixed amount. The Securities Investor Protection Corporation (SIPC) provides no insurance against loss. Securities investments, by their very nature, pose a risk of loss that an investor must consider prior to making any investment. The SIPC does not restore funds that investors lose through poor investments, even if the investor is the victim of fraud. The SIPC only insures investors against the loss due to theft or default for securities and cash that have been entrusted with a broker-dealer. If an investor has purchased five hundred shares of a stock, the SIPC ensures that the investor is compensated if the broker-dealer steals those shares or cannot provide them to the investor due to bankruptcy; however, the investor is not protected if the shares lose value.

FEDERAL REGULATIONS TO PROTECT PRIVATE INFORMATION OF INVESTORS

The Gramm-Leach Bliley Act, also known as SEC Regulation S-P, established regulations that protect the private information of investors. Investment companies, investment advisers, and broker-dealers (as well as financial companies outside the securities industry) are required to protect their clients' confidential information. Investment advisers and broker-dealers must establish safeguards to protect their clients' nonpublic information from inadvertent disclosure, as well as establish processes that ensure the safe disposal of any client credit information they possess. Furthermore, investment advisers and broker-dealers must provide written notice of the practices they have established to protect client confidentiality to all of its individual customers. Investment advisers and broker-dealers are prohibited from disclosing any non-public information about an individual client to any nonaffiliated third party without the client's prior consent.

BANK SECRECY ACT

The Bank Secrecy Act (BSA) is also known as the Currency and Foreign Transactions Reporting Act. The BSA is federal legislation that targets broker-dealers and financial dealers that may be aiding clients attempting to launder money, evade taxes, or engage in other criminal behavior. The BSA instituted record-keeping requirements for certain cash purchases. In addition, the BSA requires broker-dealers and financial institutions to report any suspicious activities that indicate a potential attempt to launder money, evade taxes, or engage in other illegal activities. The BSA also instituted an obligation for financial institutions and broker-dealers to report any aggregate daily cash transaction in excess of ten thousand dollars. The goal of the BSA is to detect current violations and to prevent future illegal activity.

The USA Patriot Act established additional requirements designed to prevent the laundering of money by terrorist groups.

EMPLOYEE RETIREMENT INCOME SECURITY ACT

The Employee Retirement Income Security Act (ERISA) was originally adopted in 1974. The Employee Retirement Income Security Act is federal legislation that regulates the management and operation of benefit plans and private pension plans. The provisions of ERISA require those managing private pensions and benefit plans to provide proper disclosure of information to the participants in the plan and their beneficiaries. ERISA also established standards outlining specific responsibilities for those managing such plans. Failure to comply with the provisions of the Employee Retirement Income Security Act may result in court actions, financial remedies, and/or ordered sanctions. The provisions of ERISA do not apply to government benefit plans or public pension plans.

REGULATION OF FINANCIAL INSTITUTIONS

Although financial institutions perform some functions that are similar to those of a broker-dealer, financial institutions are not considered broker-dealers. Financial institutions are not regulated by the Uniform Securities Act. Instead, the activities of financial institutions are governed by other legislation and/or federal regulations. Banks and savings and loan institutions are widely understood to be financial institutions; however, these are not the only entities that qualify as financial institutions. Other types of financial institutions include entities such as insurance companies, pension trusts, trust companies, institutional buyers, and profit-sharing trusts. The Uniform Securities Act excludes all of these financial institutions from the definition of broker-dealer. As such, these companies do not fall under the jurisdiction of the Administrator.

REQUIREMENTS FOR REQUEST TO REGISTER SECURITY WITH STATE ADMINISTRATOR

Many securities must be registered with the state Administrator. If a security must be registered, a registration statement must be filed with the Administrator. The registration statement for the security must note the size of the security offering and the quantity offered in the Administrator's state. The registration statement must also identify any other states in which the security will be offered. In addition, the registration statement for the security must disclose any unfavorable rulings concerning the offering made by any court, state Administrator, or other agency regulating securities in any state or federal jurisdiction. Finally, the appropriate filing fee must accompany the registration statement for the security. Once the Administrator receives all of the necessary documentation and associated fees, the Administrator will review the filing. If everything is found to be in order, the Administrator will register the security.

IMPACT OF NSMIA OF 1996 ON STATE REGULATION OF FEDERALLY REGULATED SECURITIES

The National Securities Markets Improvement Act of 1996 (NSMIA) established a clear division of responsibilities between state and federal regulators for the regulation of securities. Under the provisions of the NSMIA, a state Administrator may not regulate a security that is federally regulated. For example, a state Administrator may not regulate a security that is already regulated by the Securities and Exchange Commission (SEC). A security that is governed by federal regulations is called a federally covered security. Before the NSMIA became effective, there were instances in which the jurisdictional distinction between state and federal securities regulators was unclear. In some instances, state and federal securities regulations overlapped, creating the potential for both conflict and duplication of effort. The NSMIA, however, establishes separate jurisdictional responsibilities for the state and federal regulators.

FEDERALLY COVERED SECURITIES

There are a number of factors that may result in a particular security being deemed a federally covered security. One of the more easily understood concepts applies to securities that trade on a national level. Securities that trade on a national level (for example, on the New York Stock exchange) involve interstate trade. Interstate transactions fall under the province of the federal government, so these securities are federally covered. In addition, for the issuers of the securities discussed above, any additional securities with greater or equal seniority to a nationally traded federally covered security are also considered federally covered security. Finally, securities that are issued by investment companies that are covered by the Investment Company Act of 1940 are federally covered securities. The issuers of these securities are federally regulated, so it reasonably follows that their securities should be federally regulated as well.

Federally covered securities include securities that are traded (or that are authorized to be traded) on the New York Stock Exchange, the American Stock Exchange, or the National Market segment of NASDAQ. Any security that is traded on a national exchange that the Securities Exchange Commission (SEC) determines is substantively similar to the exchanges listed above is also considered a federally covered security. Other federally covered securities include securities issued by a municipal or other government issuer located outside the state where the securities are offered; securities that are only offered to the issuer's existing securities owners where no commissions (or other form of compensation) applies to the solicitation of the exchange of security; and securities offered by an issuer that is registered (or that has filed a registration statement) under the Investment Company Act of 1940 (although federally covered, states may require a notice filing for investment company securities).

SECURITIES EXEMPT FROM STATE REGISTRATION

A number of the securities that are considered exempt from registration with the state Administrator are exempt due to the fact that another governing body is responsible for the security in question. The following types of securities are exempt from registration with the state: securities that are issued, guaranteed, or otherwise insured by the government of the United States (including securities issued by the United States Treasury); securities that are issued, guaranteed, or otherwise insured by state or municipal governments; securities that are issued, guaranteed, or otherwise insured by any governmental body in Canada (whether local or federal); and securities that are issued, guaranteed, or otherwise insured by the federal government of any country with which the United States maintains diplomatic relations. Although these securities are exempt from registration, state Administrators may require the issuer to pay filing fees normally associated with registration.

Many securities issued by persons that are subject to alternative governance or regulation are exempt from registration with the state Administrator. These state-exempt securities include securities issued and/or guaranteed by a bank, savings institution, trust company, savings and loan, building and loan, credit union, or an international bank. These also include securities issued and/or guaranteed by an insurance company to finance a debt. Exempt insurance company securities include any insurance company-offered stocks and/or bonds, but do not include insurance policies that do not constitute securities. Exempt securities also include securities issued by a utility or company that is government by the Interstate Commerce Commission or the Public Utility Holding Company Act of 1935, including railroad securities, common carrier securities, public utilities, and public utility holding company securities. Finally, federally covered securities are also exempt from state registration.

A number of securities that are not government issued or subject to alternative regulation are nevertheless exempt from regulation due to the nature of the security. These securities include securities issued by non-profit organizations such as churches, schools, athletic clubs, and other charitable institutions. Securities offered in the form of investment contracts issued in connection with an employee benefit plan, such as a stock option plan, pension plan, savings plan, or other employee profit-sharing plan, are also exempt from registration. Finally, securities issued as a promissory note that have a minimum worth of at least $50,000 and that receive one of the three highest possible rates from a nationally recognized statistical rating firm qualify for registration exemption if the promissory note matures within 270 calendar days (nine months) of issuance.

ENFORCING ANTI-FRAUD PROVISIONS OF UNIFORM SECURITIES ACT

The Uniform Securities Act grants state Administrators the power to enforce securities fraud even if the security in question is exempt from registration or is registered with the Securities and Exchange Commission (SEC). A security's exemption from the requirement to register with the state Administrator does not mean that the anti-fraud provisions of the Uniform Securities Act no longer apply. In fact, the anti-fraud powers granted to the state Administrator by the Uniform Securities Act apply to all securities and securities transactions that occur within the state. This means that the state Administrator has the authority to deal with fraudulent securities and fraudulent securities transaction within the state regardless of whether the security in question is registered with the state, a federally covered security, or a security that does not have to be registered with the SEC or the state Administrator.

IMPACT ON REQUIREMENTS FOR REGISTRATION OF PERSONS

An exempt security is a security that does not have to be registered. If an issuer only deals with exempt securities, the representatives of that agency are not agents and need not be registered as agents with the Administrator as long as there is no compensation associated with the transaction. However, if an issuer has both registered securities and exempt securities, any representatives for the issuer that deal with the registered securities must be registered agents. A variety of securities are considered exempt. Examples of exempt securities include federal and municipal securities; securities for domestic banks, savings and loan institutions, and trust companies; and securities associated with the investment contracts for various employee investments such as employee pension plans and employee stock purchases.

LOSS OF EXEMPTION STATUS

There are two types of exempt securities that are generally exempt that may lose their right to exemption. The first are securities issued by non-profit organizations such as churches, schools, athletic clubs, and other charitable institutions. The second are securities offered in the form of investment contracts issued in connection with an employee benefit plan such as a stock-option plan, pension plan, savings plan, or other employee profit-sharing plan are also exempt from registration. The individual issuers of these types of securities may at times lose their exemption and be required to register any securities that they issue. As a result, although these types of securities do not have to be registered with the state Administrator under normal circumstances, it is important to be aware that these issuers may lose their exemption status.

EXEMPT SECURITIES TRANSACTIONS THAT MAY BE CONDUCTED BY REGISTERED AGENTS

If an issuer's security registered under the Securities Exchange Act of 1934, or is registered under the Investment Company Act of 1940, or if the issuer has filed information substantively similar to that required for either the Securities Exchange Act of 1934 or the Investment Company Act of 1940 with the state Administrator and has maintained that information for 180 days, agent-managed transactions involving the security may be exempt. Transactions for such securities handled by an agent are considered exempt if the transaction in question is a transaction between non-issuers, as long as the security in question has been in the possession of the public (not the issuer) for a minimum of ninety days.

EXEMPT SECURITIES TRANSACTIONS BETWEEN NON-ISSUERS

Unsolicited, non-issuer, client-initiated securities transactions that are handled by a broker-dealer are considered exempt transactions. Similarly, non-issuer transactions between foreign non-issuing parties are considered exempt transactions. Isolated securities transactions between two non-issuers are also considered exempt, whether handled privately or by a broker-dealer. For example, if a broker-dealer has a non-issuer client that wishes to sell its holdings, and the same broker-dealer has another non-issuer client that wishes to buy the holdings of the first client, that securities transaction is considered exempt. In order to qualify for exemption, the issuer of the security may not be a recipient of the proceeds associated with the transaction, and the act of trading itself must not be a regular practice for the seller or purchaser involved.

Non-issuer initiated securities transactions may qualify for exempt status based upon the issuer's own reporting requirements or the type of security in question. For example, if the issuer of the security in question is required to file reports with the Securities and Exchange Commission (SEC), any non-issuer transactions for the issuer's securities are considered exempt transactions. Non-issuer transactions involving particular types of fixed-income securities are also considered exempt transactions; however, in order to qualify for exempt status, the issuer of the fixed-income security must not be bankrupt or currently involved in reorganization. In addition, securities transactions between non-issuers in which the security is transferred as collateral for a loan are exempt as long as the transaction is not performed specifically to exempt the transfer from the requirements of the Uniform Securities Act.

EXEMPTION FOR SECURITIES TRANSACTION OFFERED ON A LIMITED BASIS

Certain securities transactions that are only offered on a limited basis are considered exempt transactions as long as specific criteria are met. In order to qualify as an exempt transaction under this provision, the offering of the security must be private in nature and available to fewer than ten non-institutional investors within the state within the previous twelve-month period. In addition, the security must be sold based on the seller's belief that these non-institutional buyers are purchasing the security solely for investment purposes. Finally, the transaction is not considered exempt if commissions or compensation of any type are paid for the solicitation of the non-institutional buyers described above.

EXEMPTION BASED UPON THE PARTY INITIATING THE TRANSACTION

Securities transactions that are initiated by named fiduciaries are exempt. This exemption includes transactions initiated by the executor of an estate, the administrator of a trust, sheriffs and marshals, and bankruptcy trustees and receivers. This exemption is designed to ease the process for parties seeking to liquidate holdings in certain circumstances, including the death of the original owner, government seizure of property, and bankruptcy. Securities transactions conducted by institutional investors are considered exempt transactions. Institutional investors are typically associated with financial institutions and manage large sums of funds on behalf of others. For example, the person that manages the money in a pension fund or a mutual fund would be considered an institutional investor.

EXEMPT SECURITIES TRANSACTIONS RELATED TO THE ISSUER'S ORGANIZATION

Securities transactions between two parties involved in a merger, reorganization, or consolidation may be exempt transactions. In order to qualify for exemption under this provision, both the issuer and the other party involved in the transaction must be parties in the merger, reorganization, or consolidation. The transaction also qualifies as exempt if the parent company or a subsidiary of the non-issuing party involved in the transaction is the entity involved in the merger, reorganization, or consolidation with the issuer of the security. Similarly, securities transactions for offering of pre-organization certificates are considered exempt transactions if there are no more than ten subscribers in total. In order to be classified as an exempt securities transaction under this provision, no commissions or other compensation can be paid for the solicitation of the transaction, and no subscriber may make any payment for the offering.

INSTANCES IN WHICH EXEMPT TRANSACTIONS DO NOT ELIMINATE THE NEED TO REGISTER A SECURITY

Issuers are not required to register non-exempt securities (securities that do not qualify for exemption from registration) if the transactions for the security that will take place qualify as exempt transactions. However, even if a particular securities transaction qualifies as an exempt transaction, registration is still required for the security involved in the transaction if the security is part of any non-exempt transactions. For example, securities transactions between the issuer and the underwriters (and amongst the underwriters) are exempt securities transactions. If the only securities transactions that occur are transactions between the issuer and the underwriters, the security does not have to be registered. However, if a public offering will be made (in addition to the transactions between the issuer and underwriters), that is not an exempt transaction. In this instance, the security must be registered even though some of the planned transactions involving the security are considered exempt.

ADDITIONAL EXEMPT SECURITIES TRANSACTIONS

Transactions in which issuers transfer securities to their own underwriters are exempt. Offerings made to existing security holders may qualify as exempt transactions. Such offerings qualify as exempt transactions if the offerings are made only to the issuer's existing security holders, and if no compensation or commission is paid for the solicitation of the transaction. Transactions in which a secured bond security is backed by either a deed of trust or a real mortgage qualify as exempt transactions as long as the whole deed of trust or real mortgage is offered with the bond as a package deal. Transactions that consist of an offer to rescind a previous, improper security transaction are considered exempt. Finally, transactions that consist of an offer to sell (or the sale of) a security to a person that resides outside of the state, and who is not present in the state, are exempt transactions.

REGISTRATION REQUIREMENTS FOR SECURITIES SUBJECT TO EXEMPT TRANSACTIONS

There are instances in which a non-exempt security does not need to be registered with the state Administrator. A non-exempt security is any security that does not qualify for exemption from registration with the state Administrator due to the identity of the issuer or type of security. A non-exempt security need not be registered with the state Administrator if the non-exempt security will only be used as part of exempt transactions. Certain securities transactions are considered exempt under the provisions of the Uniform Securities Act due to the nature of the transaction. If all of the transactions involving the security in question are exempt transactions, then the security need not be registered with the state Administrator. However, it should be noted that the anti-fraud provisions of the Uniform Securities Act continue to apply for such unregistered securities and transactions. Issuers must demonstrate that the transaction in question is exempt.

REGISTRATION OF SECURITIES BY QUALIFICATION FILING

For a securities issuer to file by qualification, it must file a consent to service of process and an application. This includes all securities that are not filed in conjunction with other filing requirements (i.e., registration by coordination, and notice filing). The application must contain the following information: the name, address, structure, and nature of the business; information pertaining to officers, directors, and all major shareholders (those holders with more than 10 percent of the outstanding shares); a description of the issuers' debt to equity; an estimate of how much capital is to be raised by the offering and to what use the funds will be put; the type of securities offered; the price of the securities; costs associated with underwriting and selling the issue; any stock options that may be created due to the issue; a copy of the prospectus and any sales handouts; a sample of the security; a legal opinion regarding the legality of the issue; and a current balance sheet from the issuer that has been audited by a third party.

ISOLATED NON-ISSUER TRANSACTIONS

An isolated non-issuer transaction is a securities transaction that occurs infrequently and is unassisted by investment professionals. The transactions are effected on an investor-to-investor basis, and no broker-dealers or agents are involved. These transactions are only initiated and participated in by individual investors. Since there are no licensed investment professionals involved in the transaction (thus no commissions paid), the originating issuer is not receiving any of the funds exchanged, and the occurrence is so infrequent, the Administrator has no oversight over the process. The definition of "infrequent" varies by state, but as a general rule there must be very few transactions per year. A breakdown of the term is explained by the infrequency (isolated nature) of the transactions, and the fact that the issuer (non-issuer) receives no proceeds.

UNSOLICITED BROKERAGE TRANSACTIONS

An unsolicited brokerage transaction is a securities transaction in which a retail investor initiates the transaction by contacting (usually by phone) her registered representative or the broker-dealer directly. It is important to distinguish a phone initiation via live contact from a message left for the agent. Live contact orders via phone are acceptable, whereas phone messages are considered outdated as soon as they are left with the answering service. Unsolicited brokerage transactions are the most common of exempt transactions. When an unsolicited order is placed, the transaction exempts the securities involved from state registration under the Uniform Securities Act (USA). The state Administrator may rule that the unsolicited order be recorded on a trade ticket that is signed by the client acknowledging that the order is unsolicited, and require that the broker-dealer keep the signed form for a certain period of time.

REGISTRATION PROCESS FOR SECURITIES AT THE STATE LEVEL

When a person desires to register a security for offering within a state (usually the issuer of the security), he is referred to as a registrant. He must obtain an application (or a registration form) from the Administrator. On the application, the registrant must inform the Administrator as to the size of offering of the securities (in that state only), other states in which the offering will be made, and if there have been judgments or orders by other authorities negatively affecting the issue. The registrant must then submit a filing fee required by the Administrator. This helps the Administrator offset administrative costs associated with the process. The fee is usually calculated as a percentage of the total offering. The Administrator may also, at his or her discretion, require ongoing reports to be filed to keep information about the issue current, require new or unusual offerings to be held in escrow, and dictate the security be sold on a special subscription form to be filed with the Administrator.

EXEMPT SECURITIES FROM STATE REGISTRATION

Due to the inherent nature of some securities offered, these securities are exempt from state registration with the Administrator. These securities include: securities issued by, guaranteed by, or the debt obligation of a financial institution (banks, credit unions, trust companies, etc.); foreign government securities; securities issued by the United States or Canadian federal governments or municipalities; insurance company securities; specific money market instruments such as banker's acceptances and commercial paper; securities issued by cooperatives; investment contracts of employee benefit plans; issues of nonprofit organizations; public utility securities (securities issued by public utilities or their holding companies, railroad-issued equipment trust certificates, and other common carrier securities issued by the US or Canadian government); and federal covered securities.

Remedies and Administrative Provisions

ADMINISTRATOR'S AUTHORITY

CONCERNING MAKING, AMENDING, AND RESCISSION OF RULES AND ORDERS

The Uniform Securities Act (USA) gives the state securities Administrator the power to make, amend, and rescind securities rules and orders. This power allows the Administrator to more effectively administer the USA by issuing rules and orders according to the way in which the Administrator interprets the USA. Although the Administrator has the authority to make these changes, he or she may not change the actual law. When exercising this power, the Administrator must publish changes, creation, and rescissions of precedent rules and orders. Rules differ from orders in that they are for all regulated persons to observe, whereas an order is specific to a person. A person who is affected by an order may challenge that order for up to sixty days after its issue.

CONCERNING CONDUCTING INVESTIGATIONS AND ISSUING SUBPOENAS

The Uniform Securities Act (USA) gives the state securities Administrator the power to conduct investigations and issue subpoenas. This is a very broad power and the Administrator may exercise it as he or she sees fit. The Administrator may choose to keep the investigation private or make it public. The location of the offense and investigation is immaterial if the infraction occurred against someone or pertaining to some security or transaction under the Administrator's jurisdiction. This allows state securities Administrators to conduct investigations across state lines. To facilitate the Administrator in executing the investigation, he or she may:

- require statements of involved parties that are given in writing and under oath
- subpoena witnesses and require their testimony
- take evidence and examine records
- publish the factual findings of the proceedings.

CONCERNING CONTUMACY

Contumacy is the failure of a person to appear before or provide evidence to the Administrator when subpoenaed. Since the Administrator has no legal authority to detain the offending person, the Uniform Securities Act (USA) provides for the event by allowing the Administrator to request the help of the court in his or her state. The court may then issue an order to the person to appear before the Administrator and supply any evidence requested. With the issuance of the legal order comes the weight of the state's justice system. If the person continues to ignore the order, he or she can (and usually will) be held in contempt of court. Contempt of court charges can lead to fines and jail time. So, while the Administrator has no power to correct contumacy, he or she may request that the state court system do so.

CONCERNING THE ISSUANCE OF CEASE-AND-DESIST ORDERS

The Uniform Securities Act (USA) gives the state securities Administrator the power to issue cease-and-desist orders pertaining to anything that falls under his or her jurisdiction and violates the USA. When the Administrator deems that a person is either acting or about to act in a manner contrary to state securities regulations and the USA, he or she may issue a cease-and-desist order and bypass any hearing associated therewith; the person who is the subject of the order must immediately cease the practice disallowed by the order. This allows the Administrator to work based on information that an infraction may be occurring, even before a formal complaint is made. Although state securities Administrators may issue cease-and-desist orders, it is not within their legal authority to enforce such orders. They must rely on the courts to impel the person to cease the prohibited practice. The courts may issue an injunction, and then the enjoined party must cease action.

DENYING, CANCELLING, AND REVOKING REGISTRATION

The Uniform Securities Act (USA) gives the state securities Administrator the power to revoke, cancel, or deny the registrations of persons who do business in the securities industry (within that state) as well as the state registrations of any securities registered in that state. The power extends to the revocation of registered agents who represent persons transacting securities business. The Administrator may only exercise these powers if the affected person has acted against the public interest and one of the following:

- Has falsified a registration statement
- Has violated the USA
- Has a felony conviction in the past ten years
- Has a securities-related misdemeanor conviction in the past ten years
- Has been enjoined to prevent transacting
- Is insolvent
- Is practicing dishonestly
- Has had his or her registration revoked by another Administrator
- Is the subject of another legal action for violating another securities regulation
- Has failed to supervise agents
- Has not paid filing fees
- Lacks training or experience

STATE SECURITIES ADMINISTRATOR EXERCISING SUMMARY POWERS

When the Administrator is said to have acted summarily, it means he or she has given an order regarding registration (revocation or postponement) without submitting to a hearing to determine actual reason to act as such. This applies to registration of persons or securities. The administrator may create an order to prevent or revoke registration, and then must immediately inform the applying or registering person and that person's employer if it applies to the situation. Although the order may be issued without a hearing, the subject of the order may request a hearing in writing, with which the Administrator must comply. If the subject of the

order does not request a hearing, the order remains valid for as long as the Administrator deems necessary.

CAUSES AND PENALTIES LEADING TO AND ARISING FROM CRIMINAL ACTIONS

Fraud is defined as purposeful concealment, misrepresentation, or omission of material fact with the intent of deceiving another for unlawful gain. If a registered person transacts business fraudulently, he is subject to the criminal provisions of the Uniform Securities Act (USA). If an accused person is found guilty and convicted of fraud, she may be subject to fines or prison time, as the court sees fit. While the Administrator does not have the power to arrest a person accused of fraud, he or she may petition the court to issue a warrant for the arrest of the accused. The State Attorney General (AG) will then determine if a criminal violation of the USA has occurred. The AG must find that the violation of the USA, or other law, was intentional and that the registered person/persons knew they were practicing fraudulently.

ADMINISTRATOR'S JURISDICTION

The Uniform Securities Act is the source of the Administrator's jurisdiction. Generally speaking, the Administrator has jurisdiction over securities transactions and the persons performing those transactions for the Administrator's state. In order for a securities transaction to fall under the Administrator's jurisdiction, the securities transaction must originate within the Administrator's state, be directed to the Administrator's state, or be accepted in the Administrator's state. The Administrator has jurisdiction over the persons conducting such transactions as well as over the transactions themselves. The Administrator has the power to adopt orders, issue rulings, issue subpoenas, and initiate and conduct investigations. In addition, the Administrator is responsible for managing the registrations for persons engaged in various securities transactions. The registration management duties of the Administrator include determining whether a party's registration should be approved, denied, suspended, or revoked.

DETERMINIATION OF JURISDICTION FOR SECURITIES OFFERED VIA BROADCAST OR PUBLICATION

Special rules apply to broadcast and published offerings. For securities offerings broadcast over radio or television, the jurisdiction for the offering is determined by the location from which the offering is broadcast. The state from which the offered broadcast originates has jurisdiction. If the broadcast is originated in State A and is received in State B, the Administrator for State B will not have jurisdiction unless the offer is accepted within State B. Similarly, if an offering is made in a newspaper or magazine that is published in State A and distributed in State B, the offering is not subject to the jurisdiction of the Administrator in State B. Finally, if an offering is made in a newspaper or magazine that is published within the state, but two thirds of the publication's circulation is out of state, the state's Administrator does not have jurisdiction over the offering.

56

ROLE OF ADMINISTRATOR

The Administrator under the Uniform Securities Act is the administrative agency, government official, or appointed representative that is responsible for handling the administration and enforcement of the Uniform Securities Act in a particular jurisdiction. The Administrator will handle the registrations and licensing in the securities industry and take action as necessary to ensure compliance. In this role, the Administrator is responsible for determining whether specific applicants qualify, and continue to qualify, to be registered or licensed. Although the Uniform Securities Act establishes a number of general functions that the Administrator will perform, the Act allows individual jurisdictions to determine the specific manner in which those functions will be performed. The role of the Administrator is to protect investors and to ensure that the public interest is served.

ESTABLISHING RULES

The Uniform Securities Act gives the Administrator the power to establish rules to promote the implementation of the Act. These rules include the following:

- The Administrator may create rules, modify existing rules, or withdraw rules.
- The Administrator must publish all of the rules (and any modifications or withdrawals) that it issues.
- The rules that the Administrator issues must be consistent with the provisions of the Uniform Securities Act.
- The rules enacted by the Administrator apply to all.
- The Administrator's rules do not amend the provisions of the Uniform Securities Act, but carry equal force in the state over which the Administrator has jurisdiction.

In short, the state's legislative body establishes the actual laws that govern securities within the state, and the Administrator establishes the rules that implement those laws. For example, the Administrator may issue a rule that establishes the specific documentation that must accompany an application for registration for an agent.

ENFORCEMENT AUTHORITY

The Uniform Securities Act grants considerable authority to the state Administrator; however, there are limits to this authority. The Administrator's primary role is to protect investors and to ensure that the public interest is served. In this role, an Administrator is permitted to issue a variety of orders supporting these goals. An Administrator may issue any of the following: a denial order, a suspension order, a revocation order, a stop order, and a cease-and-desist order. Each of these orders impact a person's rights to conduct business concerning securities within the state. Prior to issuing any order other than a cease-and-desist order, the Administrator must first allow the other party an opportunity to present its case in a hearing. That party has 60 days to appeal orders impacting a license (denial orders, suspension orders, and revocation orders).

POWER TO ISSUE CEASE-AND-DESIST ORDERS

One of the powers of the Administrator is the ability to prevent an anticipated violation of the Uniform Securities Act. If the Administrator has found that a violation is about to occur, it may issue a cease-and-desist order. The Administrator is not required to hold a hearing prior to issuing such an order. A cease-and-desist order prohibits a specific party from engaging in a particular activity. The Administrator's power to issue cease-and-desist orders enables the Administrator to proactively protect investors instead of merely reacting after the violation has already occurred. Although the Administrator does not have the authority to enforce a cease-and-desist order, if a party ignores the Administrator's cease-and-desist order, the Administrator may petition a court to issue an injunction against the party.

INVESTIGATORY AUTHORITY

The Administrator has been given the authority to perform investigations necessary to ensure compliance with the Uniform Securities Act. As part of its investigatory authority, the Administrator may issue subpoenas and require involved parties to produce relevant documentation and other evidence. The Administrator's investigative authority is not limited to the state over which the Administrator has jurisdiction; however, another state's Administrator may help in the enforcement of an out-of-state subpoena. Generally speaking, the results of the Administrator's investigation will be public; however, the results may remain private in certain instances if special treatment is deemed justified. The Administrator may require witnesses to provide sworn testimony and/or affidavits regarding facts relating to the investigation. The powers of the Administrator enable the Administrator to resolve complaints and effectively implement the provisions of the Uniform Securities Act.

MAKING RESTITUTION IF SECURITY IS SOLD IN VIOLATION OF UNIFORM SECURITIES ACT

If a party discovers that it has sold a security in a manner that violates the provisions of the Uniform Securities Act, it can avoid a lawsuit by offering to purchase the security back from the purchaser at the original price plus interest. The Administrator determines the amount of interest that must be included in the offer. In addition, the offer will enable the purchaser to recover reasonable attorney's fees associated with the offer. Any income the purchaser received from the security is deducted from the amount of the offer. Extending an offer of this type is called offering the right of rescission to the buyer. Such offerings may be made through a letter of rescission. The buyer has thirty days to accept the offer. If the buyer does not accept the offer, the buyer gives up the right to file a lawsuit on the matter.

CANCELING AND WITHDRAWING REGISTRATION

In addition to the power to deny, suspend, or revoke a party's registration, Administrators also have the power to cancel registration. A canceled registration is not grounds for a future denial, suspension, or revocation of registration and does not carry a penalty. An Administrator may cancel a party's registration if the Administrator determines that the registrant has ceased to exist (is no longer considered to be a legal person) or is no longer conducting business in the state. A registered party also has the option of withdrawing its own registration without penalty as long as the Administrator has not already initiated a proceeding to suspend or revoke the registration. A withdrawn registration will not prevent the party from obtaining registration in the future. If a party requests the withdrawal of its registration, the withdrawal will become effective thirty days after the application for withdrawal is received.

FRAUD AND ASSOCIATED CRIMINAL PENALTIES

Fraudulent securities transactions may result in criminal charges. For fraud to occur, it is not enough for a person to provide misleading or false information during a securities transaction. The activity is not considered fraudulent unless the person deliberately acted in a manner designed to mislead. For example, assume that an agent informed a client that a merger was likely to occur and would probably lead to an increase in the value of a particular investment in the near future. Additionally, assume that the agent was aware that there were significant hurdles that might prevent the merger from occurring, but the agent withheld this information from the client in order to promote the sale. Withholding this information is fraudulent behavior. The statute of limitation for such criminal offenses under the Uniform Securities Act is five years and may carry a maximum penalty of $5,000 and/or up to three years in prison.

RESTITUTION FOR INVESTMENT ADVICE PROVIDED IN VIOLATION OF UNIFORM SECURITIES ACT

Investment advisers that provide investment advice that violates the provisions of the Uniform Securities Act are liable to any clients that purchased securities based on that advice. An investor that purchases securities based on advice provided by an investment adviser in violation of the Uniform Securities Act is entitled to receive compensation from the investment adviser. Specifically, an investment adviser that has provided such inappropriate investment advice is liable to pay compensation to its purchasing clients for the fee associated with the inappropriate advice (along with Administrator-determined interest), any losses the client has incurred based on the advice, and reasonable attorney's fees. The investment adviser is not liable for the purchase price its client paid for the securities themselves.

AUTHORITY OVER INVESTMENT ADVISERS NOT REGISTERED WITH THE STATE

Investment advisers are held accountable to the state Administrator for any fraudulent or deceptive business practices even if the investment adviser is not otherwise subject to registration and regulation by the state. For example, even if an investment adviser is federally registered, the state Administrator still has the authority to take action if the investment adviser defrauds, misleads, or deceives clients within the Administrator's state. The fact that the investment adviser is not registered with the state Administrator does not preclude the Administrator from taking action in such circumstances. The state Administrator has the power and authority to enforce the rules governing fraud occurring within the state regardless of whether the investment adviser (or a party acting as an investment adviser) is required to register with the state Administrator.

CIVIL PENALTIES FOR VIOLATORS OF UNIFORM SECURITIES ACT

An investor may initiate civil proceedings if the investor is the victim of a security transaction that violates the provisions of the Uniform Securities Act or the implementing rules or orders of the Administrator. A lawsuit may be filed if the investor purchased securities that were not sold in accordance with the Uniform Securities Act or from an unregistered agent. An investor also has the right to sue if he or she is the victim of fraud. In order to file such a lawsuit, the investor must initiate proceedings within two years of the investor's discovery of the violation, or within three years from the date that the investor purchased the security or received the advice the advice at issue, whichever is earlier.

OFFER AND SALE AS APPLICABLE TO ANTI-FRAUD PROVISIONS

The anti-fraud provisions of the Uniform Securities Act apply to all offers and sales of securities. An offer includes any attempt to make a security available to another party. This includes completed sales; contracts agreeing to a sale; direct offers in which one person indicates that he or she is willing to sell (or otherwise dispose of) a security at a given price; and also to more indirect offers, referred to as the solicitation of an offer to buy, in which one person does not make an offer, but attempts to incite another person to make an offer. The Uniform Securities Act defines the terms sale and offer broadly to ensure that people cannot avoid the anti-fraud provisions that apply to the offer, sale, or purchase of a security by framing the transaction in a manner that would not typically be considered an offer or a sale.

REQUIRED INFORMATION REGISTRATION WITH ADMINISTRATOR

The precise information required for registration is determined by the Administrator for the state. Required information may include the type and location of the desired business, the requesting party's proposed means of doing business, current qualifications, previous performance history, any negative rulings relating to securities (whether ruling is civil or criminal in nature), and financial history. The registration information will describe the individual or individuals seeking registration, the services the requesting party seeks to offer, the proposed location for the business, the legal structure of the firm, and its financial soundness. In the case of broker-dealers and investment advisers, this information may be required for any partners, associates, or directors of the requesting firm.

REGISTRATION PROCESS

Applicants must provide complete and accurate information when registering with the Administrator. A registration fee must accompany the application. Different registration fees may apply for broker-dealers, agents, investment advisers, and investment adviser representatives. These fees vary by state. If the Administrator identifies no issues with the application, the requested license will be granted at noon on the thirtieth day. If, however, the Administrator finds problems with the application, the Administrator may choose to amend or deny the application. When amending the application, the Administrator may make the license conditional on meeting certain additional requirements or place limits on the applicability of the license. If approved, the applicant must ensure that all registration is kept current. The Administrator may hold periodic unannounced inspections.

RECORD-KEEPING REQUIREMENTS AFTER REGISTRATION

Once registered with the Administrator, broker-dealers and investment advisers are required to establish and maintain certain records. The state's Administrator establishes the specific record-keeping requirements. The types of records that may be required include accounts, papers, correspondence and other records. All required records must be kept and be available for review for a period of three years (for broker-dealers) or five years (for investment advisers). All of the directors, partners, and/or officers for the broker-dealer (as well as any individual acting in a similar capacity) who are active participants in the broker-dealer's registered activities will automatically be registered as agents when the broker-dealer is registered with the Administrator unless the state's Administrator establishes a different retention period for a particular type of record.

REVIEW OF BUSINESS RECORDS

The Uniform Securities Act gives a state Administrator the authority to review the business records belonging to the broker-dealers and investment advisers registered in the state. Broker-dealer and investment adviser records may be reviewed by the Administrator or by the Administrator's representatives. The Administrator may designate representatives who are located outside the Administrator's state to review the business records. Such reviews may be scheduled to occur periodically or at any time the Administrator deems appropriate in order to protect investors or serve the public interest. Refusal to make any documents requested by the Administrator available to the Administrator (or the Administrator's designated representatives) is a violation of the Uniform Securities Act.

REGISTRATION REVIEW PROCESS

The Administrator may not deny a requesting party's licensing solely based on an applicant's lack of experience as long as the applicant has demonstrated their qualification based on training and/or demonstrated knowledge. The Administrator reviewing the qualifications of a firm seeking licensing as a broker-dealer or investment adviser may only consider the personnel or associates of the firm that are actively involved in the firm's activities involving securities. The Administrator may not consider personnel that work for the firm, or individuals that have invested in the firm but are not involved in day-to-day activities concerning securities. For example, the Administrator may review the firm itself and any agents or investment adviser representatives it employs, but it may not review the firm's maintenance staff when considering the firm's application for licensing. Clerical staff members are only agents if they perform securities transactions.

ADMINISTRATIVE REQUIREMENTS FOR ACCEPTABLE SECURITY REGISTRATION STATEMENTS

Issues associated with the registration statement for a security may result in the suspension, revocation, or denial of registration for the security. The registration statement must be complete and accurate. The security must also be a security that is eligible for registration. If the security is ineligible, registration will not be granted. The person requesting the registration of a security must also follow the correct procedure for doing so. Failure to submit the request for registration properly will jeopardize the security's registration. Finally, the Administrator will not approve the registration of a security if the required registration fee has not been paid. In this event, the Administrator will deny the request. The Administrator may not order suspension or revocation of registration for non-payment. When registration has been denied due to non-payment, the denial will be reversed (vacated) upon receipt of the required fee.

EXAMINATION OF REQUEST FOR REGISTRATION OF A SECURITY

Administrators have been charged with the responsibility of protecting investors. One way that Administrators protect investors is by scrutinizing the registration statement for a security before allowing the security to be registered in the state. When evaluating the security's registration statement, the Administrator will consider all of the promotional materials that the security's issuer plans to use. This review helps the Administrator ensure that the offering will be presented appropriately and that the promotional materials are not misleading or unethical in any material respect. The Administrator will also consider any pertinent facts relating to the registration and/or offering of the security in other jurisdictions. Finally, the Administrator will evaluate the contractual relationship between the issuer of the security and the underwriters for the security and agreements between the underwriters. All of these steps enable the Administrator to make an educated determination regarding the registration of the security.

NOTIFICATION OF INTENT TO DENY, SUSPEND, OR REVOKE REGISTRATION OF THE SECURITY

If a state Administrator intends to issue an order to deny, suspend, or revoke the registration of a security, the Administrator must first provide notice of its intent and the Administrator's written findings of fact and conclusions of law to the issuer of the security. Upon receipt of such notice, the issuer of the security has the right to contest the finding by requesting a hearing. Although an Administrator cannot issue an order to deny, suspend, or revoke the registration of a security without providing advanced notice, the Administrator may exercise its right to issue an emergency cease-and-desist order if the situation warrants such treatment. If necessary, the Administrator also has the ability to issue a type of temporary suspension pending the outcome of the hearing. These provisions are designed to ensure that the issuer receives fair treatment while enabling the Administrator to protect investors.

NOTICE FILING METHOD OF REGISTRATION

The notice filing method for registering a security with a state Administrator (also known as registration by notification or registration by filing) is similar to the process for registration by coordination. Both processes are means by which an issuer may register a security that must be registered with the SEC with a state administrator. The notice filing method of registration is only available to issuers that have been in business for a minimum of three years. Eligible issuers must also have filed all reports required by the SEC during the previous three years. In addition, the notice filing method of registration may not be used if the issuer has been in default at any time during the current fiscal year for the payment of any owned principal, interest, or dividends. The issuer must also meet additional minimum criteria for firm size net worth.

Communications with Clients and Prospects

MATERIAL FACTS IN SECURITIES TRANSACTIONS

It is illegal for any person to intentionally make any false or misleading statements regarding any material fact when selling or purchasing a security. Such conduct is considered an act of fraud and is prohibited for registered and unregistered persons alike. A material fact is any piece of information that a potential investor relies upon when deciding whether or not to invest. While information directly relating to the value of the security itself is considered material fact, the definition of material fact is much broader. The experience and reputation of a broker-dealer may be a material fact if a potential investor relies on that experience and reputation when making an investment decision. Any information, whether directly related to the security or not, that the investor considers as part of the investment decision is a material fact.

MARKET PERFORMANCE

The historical or projected performance of a security involved in a securities transaction is considered a material fact. If an agent implied that a particular security had experienced good performance year after year, when in reality the security was issued only a year ago, the agent would be providing false information concerning a material fact. Similarly, if the agent told a potential investor that a particular security issued yearly dividends that average a specific amount per share, but neglected to inform the investor that future dividends were expected to be much smaller, the agent would have omitted a material fact. If the agent provided such false or misleading information knowingly, the agent would have committed fraud in violation of the Uniform Securities Act.

COMPANY'S HISTORICAL PERFORMANCE

Material facts include all information that may influence a client's investment decisions. This includes information that may impact the client's decision to purchase or sell a security as well as information that may impact the volume of a particular security the client may choose to buy or sell. All of these factors must be considered when determining which facts are material facts. Material facts relating to a company's historical performance may include information such as historical trends in the company's stock price, the company's historical financial performance (including profits, losses, revenues, and expenses), the company's current goals and historical success in meeting its performance goals, and the company's historical payment of dividends to shareholders (if any). The previous list should not be viewed as all-inclusive. An historical fact is a material fact if it is likely to influence an investment decision.

FACTS REGARDING SECURITIES PROFESSIONAL

Any fact that would tend to make a client feel comfortable (or uncomfortable) relying upon the advice of a securities professional is a material fact. For example, if an agent kept Harvard memorabilia in his office, and informed clients that he or she went to Harvard, when, in truth, the agent did not attend Harvard, but had been to Harvard occasionally to visit a friend, the agent would be committing fraud by omitting material facts. The agent did not make an untrue statement when by saying he or she went to Harvard, but did mislead clients by implying he or she attended Harvard as a student. It is fraudulent for any securities professional to provide dishonest or misleading information regarding their knowledge, expertise, experience, or training to their clients.

SHARING INFORMATION REGARDING FUTURE LISTING OF A SECURITY

A broker-dealer or agent may not provide information to a client, or a potential client, regarding an upcoming change in the list for a particular security unless the broker-dealer or agent knows with certainty that the change in listing will occur in the near future. This type of information is considered a material fact. A change in the listing of a security may cause an increase in the security's market value, and it may provide an indication of the anticipated future performance of the security. It is unethical and fraudulent for an agent or broker-dealer to inform a client that such a change is pending based on speculation. If the agent or broker-dealer does not have specific knowledge of the change as a factual matter, the agent or broker-dealer is prohibited from informing a client that such a change is pending.

TRUTHFUL REPRESENTATION OF CLIENT ACCOUNTS

Broker-dealers and agents must be truthful in their representations regarding their clients' accounts. Account statements provided by the broker-dealer or agent must not include false information or be intentionally misleading. In addition, any discussions between the broker-dealer or agent and the client regarding the account must be truthful and accurate. It is fraudulent for a broker-dealer or agent to attempt to mislead a client in any way regarding the status of the client's account. If a client has suffered a loss, the broker-dealer or agent must not attempt to hide this fact from the client or otherwise mislead the client. Such behavior is considered a misstatement or omission of a material fact, and, if done intentionally, is considered an act of fraud subject to criminal charges.

COMMITMENT TO AGREEMENT OF PROVISION OF SERVICES

The Uniform Securities Act prohibits a broker-dealer or agent from committing to providing a service to a customer without in fact providing it. In addition, the Uniform Securities Act prohibits a broker-dealer or agent from agreeing to perform services for its clients that it is not qualified to perform. Such action is considered fraud and is prohibited by the Uniform Securities Act. For example, if a client asked an agent to provide a particular type of analysis comparing several securities, and the agent promised to do so, it would be considered fraudulent if the agent either did not intend to perform the promised analysis, or did not have the knowledge or training necessary to effectively perform the analysis. In either case, the agent

would be committing an act of fraud by telling the client it would perform the analysis in question.

INVESTMENT RECOMMENDATIONS

CONSIDERATION OF CLIENT'S INVESTMENT OBJECTIVES

Agents must consider their clients' best interests when making investment recommendations. In order to meet this obligation, agents must ask their clients for pertinent information before making any recommendation. The information that agents must request from their clients includes information regarding current finances, investment goals, and need for investment stability. These three factors will help the agent determine the amount of investment the client can reasonably afford, the types of securities that are best able to meet the clients investment goals (e.g., growth or income), and the appropriate mix of high-risk and low-risk investments for the particular client. Any securities transactions that the agent recommends must meet these client-driven factors. The Uniform Securities Act prohibits agents from recommending a securities transaction for a client that is inconsistent with the client's investment objectives.

INSIDE INFORMATION

The Uniform Securities Act prohibits persons from using material inside information to make investment recommendations. Inside information includes any facts that could potentially impact the value of a security but that are not currently publicly available. For example, assume that an agent had a close relative who was negotiating a large contract with a company with a publicly offered stock. Further assume that because of the agent's personal relationship, the agent was aware that the contract was very likely to be consummated in the near future and that the consummation of the contract would likely cause a significant rise in the company's stock price. This type of information is considered material inside information. The agent must inform a supervisor that the he or she possesses the information, and the agent is prohibited from making investment recommendations based on this information.

GUARANTEEING A SECURITY'S PERFORMANCE

The Uniform Securities Act prohibits persons acting as securities professionals from making guarantees regarding the performance of securities to its clients. Under this provision of the Uniform Securities Act, the type of guarantee that is prohibited is any guarantee regarding the future performance of the security in terms of principal return, dividends, or interest. However, it should be noted that while a security professional may not make any such guarantee, the professional may reference an existing guarantee applying to a security if a party other than the security's issuer has guaranteed the security in some way. In other words, the securities professional may not provide any guarantee against potential loss or a security's future performance; however, if another party has guaranteed the security, the securities professional is permitted to inform its client of the existence of the guarantee.

DOCUMENTATION OF INVESTOR ADVISER'S RELATIONSHIP TO CLIENT

The provisions of the Uniform Securities Act governing dealer-broker and agent behavior apply to persons acting as investment advisers or investment adviser representatives; however, additional requirements apply to persons that act as investment advisers. The Uniform Securities Act requires that the relationship between an investment adviser and its clients be memorialized in a contract unless the Administrator has specifically waived this requirement. These contracts must meet specific criteria. First, the contracts must outline the specific fee structure. The contract must also prohibit the investment adviser from transferring the client's account to another party unless the client has agreed to the transfer. For partnerships, the provisions must require the investment adviser to notify the client if there is a change of partners. Finally, the investor adviser must disclose at least 49 hours prior to finalizing the contract any relevant legal activities occurring in the last ten years in which it has been involved.

INFORMING CLIENTS OF INVESTMENT ADVISER'S BENEFIT IF CLIENT TAKES INVESTMENT ADVISER'S ADVICE

Investment advisers are required to inform their clients if they are recommending that the clients take any action that is likely to benefit the investment adviser. For example, if an investment adviser owned a significant number of shares in a particular security, the investment adviser would stand to gain if its clients purchased a large number of shares for the same security and drove up the security's market value. As a result, if an investment adviser does own a significant number of shares in a particular security, the investment adviser is required to inform its clients of the potential conflict of interest when advising its clients to invest in the security. Withholding this information from clients is prohibited under the provisions of the Uniform Securities Act.

DISCLOSURE OF THIRD PARTY ANALYSIS

Investment advisers are required to inform clients any time they rely on reports prepared by third parties. This means that an investment adviser cannot take credit for analysis performed by someone else and must reveal the source of any analysis performed by others, and upon which the investment adviser relies, to the client. The exception to this prohibition is when the investment relies upon documentation prepared by a third party that is merely statistical. For example, if the investment adviser used a statistic report authored by a third party to aid its analysis, the investment adviser would not need to inform the client that it used a third party provided report; however, if the investment adviser used analysis prepared by another party as part of its own analysis, the adviser would need to disclose this information to its client.

INVESTMENT ADVISER'S RESPONSIBILITY TO DISCLOSE SOURCE OF THIRD-PARTY RECOMMENDATIONS AND REPORTS

Investment advisers are permitted to provide both reports and investment recommendations prepared by other parties to their clients. However, investment advisers that engage in this type of activity must provide proper disclosure to their

Copyright © Mometrix Media. You have been licensed one copy of this document for personal use only. Any other reproduction or redistribution is strictly prohibited. All rights reserved. This content is provided for test preparation purposes only and does not imply an endorsement by Mometrix of any particular political, scientific, or religious point of view.

client. If an investment adviser provides a report or recommendation to a client that was prepared by another party, the investment adviser must inform the client that the adviser did not prepare the report or recommendation and must identify the party that did. It should be noted that the requirement to provide such disclosure does not apply if the investment adviser merely utilized a published report while conducting the research necessary to provide investment advice to the client. In short, an investment adviser cannot take credit for someone else's work, but can use research performed by others to aid the investment adviser's own research efforts.

CLIENT-SPECIFIC APPROACH TO RECOMMENDATIONS
BROKER-DEALER'S RESPONSIBILITY

Broker-dealers are expected to adhere to high ethical standards while conducting business. Prior to recommending that a client engage in the exchange, sale, or purchase of any security, a broker-dealer must have established a reasonable basis for the recommendation. In addition to ensuring that the recommendation is reasonable based upon objective data available to the broker-dealer, the broker-dealer must consider each client's unique circumstances. One size does not fit all. Broker-dealers must follow a client-specific approach. Any transactions recommended by a broker-dealer must be consistent with the client's short-term and long-term investment goals and be appropriate for the client's financial situation. In addition to these considerations, the broker-dealer must also take into account any other relevant facts of which it is aware.

INVESTMENT ADVISER'S RESPONSIBILITY

As part of an investment adviser's obligation to understand the goals of its clients, investment advisers must inform their clients when those goals are not realistic. For example, if a client wanted to invest in securities that would be very secure, provide a steady income, and experience very significant short-term growth, the investment adviser would need to explain why the client's expectations were not realistic. As part of the investment adviser's explanation, he would need to explain the risks and advantages of the various investment offerings in order to help the client understand the available options. Advising a client involves more than simply telling clients which securities are likely to provide a healthy return on an investment. Advising a client also means helping to ensure that the investment advice provided fits the client's individual needs.

OBTAINING PROPER AUTHORIZATION FROM CLIENTS

Obtaining proper authorization is an absolute must for broker-dealers. Broker-dealers may not act unless they have first obtained appropriate client authorization. Before a broker-dealer may initiate any securities transaction on behalf of a client, the broker-dealer must first secure the proper authorization for the transaction from the client. This requirement applies for all client securities transactions including, but not necessarily limited to, the purchase, sale, or exchange of securities. Broker-dealers may not act without their client's permission even if the broker-dealer believes the action would be in the client's best interest. If a broker-dealer fails to obtain proper client authorization prior to initiating a security transaction, the broker-dealer's registration may be denied, suspended, or revoked.

ACCURACY OF COMMUNICATION

Broker-dealers must ensure that all communications regarding securities transactions are accurate. This requirement applies to all communications reporting the purchase or sale of a security or securities including, but not limited to, advertisements, newspaper and periodical articles, and investment advisories. For example, an advertisement may not describe a mere offer to sell a security as though an actual sale had occurred. If the communication lists an offered sale price for a security or states an offer to purchase a security, the price contained in the communication must reflect the true price of the offer as understood by the broker-dealer. All communications must include any relevant information necessary to ensure that the communication is not misleading. In short, all broker-dealer communications relating to securities transactions should be accurate and complete.

REFERENCING MARKET PRICES ACCURATELY

Broker-dealers must be careful when claiming that a particular security is being offered at or below "market" price. The first issue a broker-dealer must consider prior to making any statement relating to a market price is whether a true outside market exists for the security in question. If the only market for the security is one that is controlled or created by the broker-dealer, then it is the broker-dealer that is establishing the price of the security, not the market. A market price only exists if the average going price for the security is out of the broker-dealer's control. In addition, the broker-dealer must ensure that it has a reasonable basis for any representations it makes regarding the current market price of a security. Misrepresenting the market price of a security may result in the suspension, revocation, or denial of a broker-dealer's registration.

RESPONSIVENESS TO CLIENTS

Broker-dealers must be responsive to their clients' requests. If a client requests that a broker-dealer provide information that the client is legitimately entitled to have, the broker-dealer must provide that information to the client within a reasonable period of time. Similarly, a broker-dealer must provide a timely response to any formal written requests submitted by its clients. Broker-dealers must also provide a response to any of its clients' written complaints. While these requirements may appear to require nothing more than good customer service, these requirements also protect investors from unscrupulous broker-dealers that would attempt to keep clients misinformed or uniformed. A broker-dealer that fails to comply with these requirements may face the suspension, denial, or revocation of its registration.

PROVIDING ACCURATE INFORMATION REGARDING QUALIFICATIONS

An investment adviser must always provide true and accurate representations to clients, and to potential clients, when describing the investment adviser's qualifications or the qualifications of any of the investment adviser's employees.

Investment advisers must also be truthful and forthcoming when describing the services that they offer, as well as when describing the fees associated with the offered services. In addition to ensuring that all statements regarding the investment adviser's qualifications, qualifications of employees, and description of services and associated fees are accurate, the investment adviser must ensure that the information provided is complete. Investment advisers may not withhold material information regarding qualifications, services, or fees from its clients or potential clients. The information provided, when considered as a whole, must be accurate and complete and must not be misleading.

GUARANTEES

Investment advisers may not provide guarantees to their clients that relate to the outcome of following the investment adviser's recommendation. For example, an investment adviser may not tell a client that if the client follows the investment adviser's investment recommendation, the client will not suffer a loss or will realize a profit. Such guarantees are strictly prohibited. Investment advisers may inform clients of the relative risk associated with any recommendation as long as the description of risk does not suggest that a security's performance is guaranteed. The act of guaranteeing investment advice is considered an unethical business practice. As with any other unethical business practice, investment advisers engaging in such inappropriate behavior may face the loss of their registration through denial, suspension, or revocation.

NEGOTIATION OF INVESTMENT ADVISORY CONTRACTS

In some industries, parties are permitted to negotiate contracts in which one party agrees to waive a right to which it would otherwise be entitled law. Investment advisers, however, are prohibited from entering into any investment advisory contract that contains provisions that would allow the investment adviser to act in a manner that is contrary to the Uniform Securities Act or the Investment Advisers Act of 1940. In other words, investment advisers are prohibited from entering into a contract with a client in which the client agrees to excuse the investment adviser from complying with one or more of its obligations. Many, if not most, of the safeguards that have been established help to protect smaller investors from potentially unscrupulous investment advisers. If investment advisers were allowed to circumvent the requirements by convincing clients to waive their rights, it would defeat the purpose for which these protections were established.

Compensation

SHARING FEES OR COMMISSIONS

The Uniform Securities Act permits registered agents for a broker-dealer to share their fees with other registered agents and to split commissions with other registered agents under some circumstances. In order for such sharing to be permissible, each agent must be registered with the state Administrator. In addition, each of the agents involved in the transaction must either be representatives for the same broker-dealer or be representatives for broker-dealers that are all controlled and/or owned by the same entity. If the individuals in question are not registered agents or do not represent registered broker-dealers that are associated with each other, the Uniform Securities Act prohibits the agents to share their fees with each other or to split any commissions between themselves.

Agents may not share their commissions or any other form of compensation associated with the sale or purchase of a security with a customer or any other non-agent. Furthermore, an agent may only split commissions (or other forms of compensation associated with the sale or purchase of a security) with agents that also represent the same broker-dealer (or directly affiliated broker-dealers). Splitting commissions (and/or other forms of compensation associated with a securities transaction) with any party other than an eligible agent is an inappropriate conflict of interest. Such behavior has been deemed unethical, and any agent that engages in such unethical behavior may have their registration denied, suspended, or revoked.

MATERIAL FACT OF TRANSACTION FEES

The amount of any fees or commissions that an agent or broker-dealer charges in connection with a security transaction is a material fact. If the transaction will result in a charge of any type, the nature of that charge must be disclosed. This is true whether the charge is applied in the form of a straight commission or in another form such as a markup. For example, it would be fraudulent for a broker-dealer or agent to inform a client, or a potential client, that no charges apply when, in fact, a charge is built in to the transaction in the form of a markup. A broker-dealer or agent must provide full disclosure to investors regarding the revenues that it will receive as a result of the transaction.

ALLOWABLE FORMS OF COMPENSATION

Investment advisers are generally prohibited from tying their compensation to the performance of their clients' securities. Under normal circumstances, investment advisers may be compensated in one of two ways: a flat fee for providing advice or a flat percentage of the assets in client's investment portfolio to be paid at specific intervals (for example, annually or quarterly). This fee structure is designed to protect average investors. However, if the investment adviser serves institutional clients (for example, investment companies) or clients that either have a net worth of at least one and a half million dollars or that have at least seven hundred and fifty

71

thousand dollars in an investment account with the firm, the investment adviser's compensation for these clients may be based on performance.

SOFT-DOLLAR COMPENSATION ARRANGEMENTS

The term "soft-dollar compensation" refers to the practice of broker-dealers providing services for which they would normally charge (such as research reports) for free to advisors in exchange for directing their business to that broker-dealer. These are referred to as directed transactions. Directed transactions can create a conflict of interest and place the advisor in direct opposition to the Investment Advisers Act of 1940 (the fiduciary responsibility). An example of such a conflict might be where the advisor directs a transaction to a broker-dealer that will not provide either the highest selling price or the lowest buying price for the client. Section 28(e) of the Securities Exchange Act of 1934 set up a "safe harbor" provision that acknowledged the value to the client of the soft-dollar reports provided to the advisors. Under Section 28(e), it is legal for the advisor to accept soft-dollar compensation, but the fact must be disclosed to the client, the client must consent, and it must be listed on the advisor's form ADV.

CHARGING PERFORMANCE-BASED FEES

Typically, under the Uniform Securities Act (USA), advisors may not charge performance-based fees; instead, fees should be based on the principal under management. There are, however, certain exceptions by which the advisor may charge performance-based fees. The investor, or qualified client, that is paying the performance-based fee must meet the following criteria:

- The person (legal or natural) must have at least $1 million dollars under management.
- Have a net worth of $2 million dollars (joint holdings with spouses may be considered to meet this requirement).
- Be a director or officer at the investment advisory firm that charges the fee, and have been employed in the securities industry for at least one year.

ETHICAL AND FIDUCIARY RESPONSIBILITY OF ADVISORS REGARDING THE CHARGING OF COMMISSIONS

For advisors to act in a fiduciary role, they must place the client's best interest ahead of their own interests. This requires that the investments recommended to the client be in their best interest, regardless of the payout to the advisor. It is unethical and a breach of fiduciary duty for an advisor to recommend an investment based on the amount of commission he or she will receive. The recommendation must be made in the client's best interest and suitable to the client's goals. Additionally, the advisor should recommend the security of lower commission of two significantly similar securities, as it is in the client's best interest to incur lower fees.

Client Funds and Securities

MARKET VALUE WHEN PROVIDING MATERIAL FACTS

One material fact that investors may rely upon when making investment decisions is a market value quotation. It is illegal to intentionally provide a client, or potential client, false information regarding the market value of a security. For example, if an agent informed a potential client that a particular stock was currently valued at twenty dollars a share when the current market value of the stock was only fifteen dollars a share, the agent would be committing fraud by making an untrue statement of a material fact. However, if an agent researched the value of a stock, and based on that research, informed a client that the market value of a stock was twenty dollars a share, when in fact, the value of the stock had dropped to fifteen dollars since the time the agent performed the research, the agent would not have acted fraudulently. Fraud cannot occur accidentally.

REPRESENTATIONS OF REGISTRATION WITH THE SEC OR ADMINISTRATOR

Persons and securities may be registered with the Securities and Exchange Commission or state Administrators. However, this registration does not mean that either the Securities and Exchange Commission or the state Administrator has approved the person or security in question. Broker-dealers and agents are prohibited from informing clients that registration with either of these regulatory bodies means that the person or security has been approved. Because an investor would be expected to consider the supposed approval by the Securities and Exchange Commission or state Administrator when making an investment decision, providing such information to a client is considered a misstatement of material fact and is an act of fraud. The Uniform Securities Act prohibits this type of misstatement. Broker-dealers or agents committing securities fraud may face criminal charges.

MAKING INVESTMENT DECISIONS ON BEHALF OF CLIENT

Agents are permitted to make certain investment decisions on behalf of their clients; however, they may only do so under very specific circumstances. Before an agent can make any investment decision on behalf of a client, the agent must first obtain written authorization from the client that gives the agent power of attorney to exercise such decisions. The agent's right to make investment decisions is limited to the specific powers granted in the written authorization. The client's authorization allows the agent to choose which securities to invest in, when to purchase a particular security and when to sell, and the amount to invest in each security. The Uniform Securities Act prohibits agents from making investment decisions on behalf of their clients without first obtaining the required written authorization from the client.

INVESTMENT RECOMMENDATIONS

Investment recommendations must always be made for the good of the client, not for the potential increase in commissions. The Uniform Securities Act requires that

73

securities professionals have a legitimate basis for making recommendations to their clients. If an agent suggests that a client invest in a particular security, that agent must have a sound reason for making the recommendation. The Uniform Securities Act also prohibits making investment recommendations in a manner designed primarily to increase commission potential. For example, agents may not recommend that a client make frequent changes to their investments in order to obtain the additional fees associated with the additional transactions. Instead, an agent's recommendations to shift investments in a client's portfolio must always be driven by what is best for the client.

MAINTAINING CUSTODY OF CLIENTS' ASSETS

Investment advisers may only maintain possession or control of their client's assets under specific circumstances. Such possession or control is referred to maintaining custody of the assets. Investment advisers may not maintain custody of their client's funds if the Administrator has issues a rule prohibiting such custody. If the Administrator has not ruled to prohibit custody, the investment adviser is obligated to inform the Administrator any time the investment adviser has custody of its client's assets. Investment advisers that maintain custody of their clients' assets are required to provide regular statements to their custodial clients that outline the value of the account, account transactions, and the location of all of the clients' assets. At a minimum, investment advisers must provide these statements to custodial clients on quarterly basis.

COMMINGLING OF CLIENT SECURITIES WITH INVESTMENT FIRM'S SECURITIES

The Uniform Securities Act requires that all of the securities owned by a client (in the client's name) be maintained in the client's individual account. The client's securities cannot be kept in the firm's own account even if records are kept that reflect the portion of the account that belongs to the client. The practice of combining a client's investment account with a firm's investment account is called commingling and is prohibited. This requirement helps ensure that firms cannot use their client's securities to gain leverage and to protect the client's investment. The commingling of client securities with a firm's securities could create the appearance that the firm actually owned far more shares of a particular stock than it truly did. Placing a client's securities in the firm's name also places the client's assets at risk in the event the firm faces financial problems.

LENDING MONEY TO CLIENTS

Investment advisers are generally prohibited from lending money to a client. Such practices are generally considered a conflict of interest. However, there are two exceptions to this provision. First, investment advisers are permitted to loan money to a client if the investment adviser is a financial institution, such as a bank, that loans money as a standard part of its business. Second, investment advisers are permitted to loan money to clients that are affiliated with the investment adviser. Investment advisers are forbidden to loan any funds to any other clients. Such action is considered an unethical business practice. Investment advisers that engage in unethical business practice may have their registration denied, suspended, or revoked by the Administrator.

BORROWING MONEY FROM CLIENTS

Investment advisers are generally prohibited from borrowing money from a client. However, there are limited exceptions to this provision. Investment advisers are permitted to borrow money from a client if the client is a financial institution that loans money as a standard part of its business (such as a bank). Investment advisers are also permitted to borrow money from a client that is a broker-dealer. Finally, investment advisers are allowed to borrow money from clients that are affiliated with the investment adviser. Investment advisers are forbidden to borrow funds from any other clients. Such action is considered an unethical business practice. Investment advisers that engage in unethical business practice may have their registration denied, suspended, or revoked by the Administrator.

BORROWING MONEY OR SECURITIES FROM CLIENTS

The Uniform Securities Act has specific provisions that place limits on a security professional's ability to borrow from clients. As a general rule, securities professional are prohibited from borrowing either securities or funds from their clients. This behavior is considered unethical and is a violation of the Uniform Securities Act. However, there are limited circumstances in which such behavior is permissible. If the client is a lending institution such as a bank or saving and loan that lends money as a standard business offering, the securities professional may borrow money from its client. Similarly, if the client is a securities firm or other business that offers securities loans as a standard business offering, the securities professional may borrow securities from the client as a customer of that client.

PROHIBITED ACTS

MATCHING PURCHASES

Matching purchases is a form of market manipulation and is prohibited by the Uniform Securities Act. Parties engaging in matching purchases are attempting to artificially increase the market value of a security. In this case, the market manipulation occurs when parties agree to repeatedly buy and sell the same security or securities to create the illusion of substantial trading activity for the security or securities. This illusion of activity is designed to entice investors to purchase shares of the security or securities and artificially drive up the market value of the security or securities. Once the market value of the security or securities has increased, the parties engaging in the matching purchases then sell their shares of the security at the artificially high price for a profit.

FRONT RUNNING

Front running is a form of market manipulation and is prohibited by the Uniform Securities Act. Front running occurs when a securities professional times investments for the securities firm in a manner that benefits the firm at the detriment of the firm's clients. For example, a large purchase or sale of shares in a particular security is likely to have an impact on the security's market price. If a firm has a client that has requested that the firm sell a large number of the client's shares in a stock, the firm cannot sell its own shares in the stock prior to selling its client's shares. Similarly, if a client wishes to purchase a large number of shares in a security, the firm cannot purchase shares in the security for its own account prior to placing its client's order in order to benefit from the resulting increase in share price.

ACCURATELY HANDLING AND RECORDING SECURITIES TRANSACTIONS

A securities professional must handle all securities transactions in an ethical manner. This requirement is very broad and is not limited by specifically identified examples of ethical and unethical behavior. A securities professional is obligated to follow the client's order specifications. Deliberately ignoring a client's instructions regarding the purchase or sale of securities is strictly prohibited. All client transactions must be accurately recorded in the broker-dealer's records unless the client has specifically requested in writing that the transaction not be recorded. In addition, the transaction record must be accurate. These requirements apply to all client transactions including private transactions. Backdating any of the records associated with a transaction is strictly prohibited, as such tactics could be use to falsify the purchase or sale price of a security. It is essential that all transactions conducted on behalf of a client be recorded properly and accurately.

MATCHING PURCHASES AND ARBITRAGE

While the practice of matching purchases is a form of market manipulation, and therefore prohibited by the Uniform Securities Act, arbitrage is permitted. When parties engage in the act of matching purchases, the parties purchase and sell securities in hopes that the sheer volume of the transactions will artificially drive up the price of the security. On the other hand, arbitrage occurs when a single party takes advantage of differing prices for the same security in different markets by buying the security in a market where it has a low price and then selling the same security in a second market where it has a higher price. Arbitrage is not a manipulation of the market. Instead, arbitrage activities help to set a realistic price for a particular security that is overvalued in one market and undervalued in another.

PROPER ACCOUNTING METHODS FOR AGENTS

Agents must always utilize proper accounting methods. Agents must ensure that each and every security transaction is properly and accurately noted in the appropriate records for the broker-dealer that the agent represents. In order to comply with this requirement, agents generally must ensure that every transaction is documented in the standard account books for the broker-dealer the agent represents. The only instance in which an agent may complete a transaction that is not recorded in the broker-dealer's standard account books is if the agent has received prior authorization, in writing, from the broker-dealer to record the transaction in a different manner. This requirement protects investors by helping to ensure that all securities transactions completed by the agent are properly tracked and recorded.

AUTHORIZATION REQUIREMENTS FOR DISCRETIONARY POWER OF INVESTMENT ADVISERS

Investment advisers are required to obtain proper authorization from the client prior to using discretionary power on behalf of the client to either order the sale of securities or the purchase of securities. Although it is probably preferable for the investment adviser to obtain the client's authorization in writing before the investment adviser exercises discretionary power on the client's behalf, prior written authorization is not required. An investment adviser may order the purchase or sale of securities on behalf of a client using discretionary power as long as the investment adviser obtained the client's verbal authorization to do so prior to the transaction. If the client's authorization of discretionary authority is provided verbally, the investment adviser is required to secure written authorization from the client within ten business days once the investment adviser has exercised its discretionary power.

FIDUCIARY RESPONSIBILITIES OF INVESTMENT ADVISERS

Investment advisers are required to act as fiduciaries. As a fiduciary, an investment adviser must place its clients' welfare above its own at all times. Although both broker-dealers and investment advisers are required to act ethically at all times, the fiduciary responsibilities of an investment adviser means that investment advisers cannot promote their own interests above the interests of their clients. For example, a broker-dealer could recommend that a client use the services of its firm for a particular securities transaction as long as the recommendation was made honestly and ethically; however, an investment adviser could not make the same recommendation if the investment adviser was aware that the client could obtain a better deal by handling the transaction differently. Both the broker-dealer and the investment adviser acted ethically in this scenario, but the broker-dealer represents itself, while the investment adviser represents the client.

AUTHORIZATION REQUIREMENTS FOR INVESTMENT ADVISERS

Investment advisers must always obtain proper client authorization prior to each and every securities transaction. Investment advisers are prohibited from placing any order on behalf of a client to purchase and/or sell securities unless the investment adviser has first obtained proper authorization from the client for the transaction in question. Although investment advisers are fiduciaries, an investment adviser may not operate without proper authorization from the client, even if the action is in the best interest of the client. Failure to obtain proper client authorization prior to initiating a securities transaction may result in the denial, revocation, or suspension of the investment adviser's registration. This prohibition also applies to instances in which the investment adviser receives instructions to initiate a securities transaction from a third party. Investment advisers may accept orders from third parties, but the investment adviser must have written authorization from the client in order to do so.

CONFIDENTIALITY OF PRIVATE INFORMATION

Investment advisers are trusted with private information belonging to their clients. It is critical that investment advisers safeguard all such private information. In order to ensure that investment advisers keep all such nonpublic information private, investment advisers must have written policies and procedures in place that outline the methods the investment adviser will use to ensure that it does not disclose nonpublic information. Investment advisers must enforce these written policies and procedures and ensure that all employees comply with these obligations. Examples of private information that must be protected include client names, client addresses, client financial information, client securities portfolios, and client-specific investment performance information. Investment advisers may not disclose this information without express permission from the client unless legally ordered to do so.

INVESTMENT ADVISORY CONTRACT STANDARDS

Investment advisers must ensure that each investment advisory contract complies with minimum standards. Investment advisory contracts must outline each of the services that the investment adviser will provide to the client. For each of the services governed by the contract, the investment advisory contract must outline the manner in which the investment adviser's fee will be calculated. The contract must also document the manner in which each fee (or portion thereof) will be refunded in the event that the contract is terminated or the investment adviser does not perform as specified. In addition, the contract must have a specified term of duration and must specify any discretionary authority the client has granted to the investment adviser. Finally, the contract must state that the investment adviser is prohibited from assigning the contract to another party without the client's express consent. Each of these requirements applies to each new, extended, or renewed investment advisory contract.

INVESTMENTS NOT CONSIDERED SECURITIES

The Uniform Securities Act does not regulate transactions that do not involve securities. Investment options offered by banks, such as certificates of deposit (CDs) insured by the FDIC, are not securities. Insurance companies also offer a number of investment options that are not considered securities, including fixed annuity offerings and various forms of life insurance (including term life insurance, whole life insurance, endowment life insurance and universal life insurance). Commodities such as gold or wheat that trade on a futures market are also excluded from the definition of securities. As such, the business practices associated with the purchase and sale of these types of investments are not governed by the Uniform Securities Act and are not subject to the authority of the state Administrator.

ETHICALLY TAKING CUSTODY OF A CLIENT'S FUNDS

Custody is defined as directly or indirectly holding or having authority to possess client funds. In order for an advisor to maintain lawful and ethical custody of a client's funds, the advisor must have a qualified custodian to maintain and hold the client's funds and security holdings in an account that is separate from other clients' funds. Additionally, the advisor must ensure that the client understands where the funds are being held in custodianship. The advisor must also make certain that the client receives a quarterly statement of account (verified by an independent public accountant), either from the custodian or from the advisor. It should be noted that the client may assign an independent representative to take delivery of the aforementioned statements.

Conflicts of Interest and Other Fiduciary Issues

FRAUD REGULATIONS

The Uniform Securities Act contains fraud regulations that are not limited to registered parties, but that instead apply to any person. A person in this context is a legal person, meaning the term includes both individuals and legal entities such as corporations, estates, or partnerships. Under these regulations, it is unlawful to engage in any activity designed to directly or indirectly defraud another party in connection with the offer, purchase, or sale of a security. For example, it would be fraudulent for a firm to imply that its investors typically realized a higher return on their investment than was in fact true. Statements are fraudulent if they contain false information on material facts or if they omit material facts that cause the statement to be misleading. Fraud occurs when a party attempts to mislead using any means.

INSIDER TRADING AND SECURITIES FRAUD ENFORCEMENT ACT OF 1998

The Insider Trading and Securities Fraud Enforcement Act of 1988 (also known as ITSFEA) is federal legislation that established more severe penalties for persons engaging in securities transactions based on material inside information. This act expanded the definition of the term *inside information* to include scenarios that were not contemplated under the Securities Exchange Act of 1934. Under the provisions of the ITSFEA, an insider is any individual (or person) who has access to corporation information that is not available to the general public. Such nonpublic information is considered inside information and may not be used by an insider, or a confidante of the insider, for purposes of making decisions regarding securities transactions. Inside information ceases to be classified as inside information once the information is made public. Once the information ceases to be inside information, the information may then be considered for future investment decisions.

INDICATIONS OF POSSIBLE MONEY LAUNDERING ACTIVITY

Securities dealers are obligated to report activity that could be tied to money laundering. The industry has identified four red flags that point to suspicious activity that should be reported:

- If the broker-dealer knows that money involved in the transaction is the result of criminal activity or that the transaction is intended to disguise illegal activity, the transaction must be reported.
- If the broker-dealer would be required to engage in criminal activity in order to complete a requested transaction, it must be reported.
- If the broker-dealer is aware that the purpose of the transaction is to circumvent the provisions of the Bank Secrecy Act, the transaction must be reported.

- The last red flag requires the broker-dealer to consider the purpose that will be served by the transaction. If the broker-dealer cannot identify a legitimate purpose for a particular transaction based on available facts, the transaction should be reported as suspicious.

ETHICAL BUSINESS PRACTICES

The Uniform Securities Act establishes standards for ethical business practices for all persons engaged in the business of issuing, buying, and/or selling securities and for all persons engaged in the business of providing investment advice regarding securities transactions. Although the provisions of the Uniform Securities Act that deal with ethical business practices are very broad, these provisions are not intended to provide an exhaustive list of prohibited behaviors. However, the Uniform Securities Act does provide many specific examples of prohibited business practices and fraudulent behaviors. The violation of the provisions concerning ethical business practices may result in the suspension, revocation, or denial of registration, and, depending upon the nature of the violation, in some cases, a violation may result in criminal charges.

COMMITTING FRAUD BY OMISSION

Omitting a material fact is a fraudulent act. Fraud by omission occurs when a person knowingly fails to share information with a client when the information in question is likely to have an impact on the client's investment decision. For example, if an agent is aware that the broker-dealer he represents has analyzed a particular stock and found that stock is currently a risky investment, but the agent chooses to withhold the results of his firm's analysis with a client, the agent is committing an act of fraud. Persons are also prohibited from making true statements if they omit key facts that are necessary to ensure the statements are not misleading. For example, it would be misleading to state that particular security had increased in value every year for the last ten years, but fail to mention that the security had been steadily losing value over the last three months.

SHARING PROFITS AND LOSSES WITH CLIENTS

As a general rule, agents cannot share a client's profits or losses; however there are certain circumstances where this is permitted. If an agent obtains prior approval from a client in writing and shares ownership of an account with a client, the agent may share profits and losses associated with the joint account with the client. In this situation, profits and losses for the joint account are shared based on the percentage of account owned by each party. For example, if the agent owns fifteen percent of the account and the client owns eighty-five percent of the account, the account's profits and loss will be split according to these percentages. Although agents are permitted to have joint accounts with their clients under the circumstances described above, broker-dealers are not. Broker-dealers are prohibited from establishing joint accounts with their clients.

PROVISIONS OF THE UNIFORM SECURITIES ACT CONCERNING RUMORS

Agents making investment recommendations to clients must base their recommendations on verifiable facts. The Uniform Securities Act prohibits agents from making investment recommendations that are based on rumors. The Uniform Securities Act also prohibits securities professionals from spreading rumors regarding securities. These requirements help to ensure that the market is driven by actual performance, not by unfounded rumors. These requirements also help to control market manipulation by unscrupulous parties. For example, assume an unethical agent spreads a rumor that the financial results for the upcoming quarter for a particular company are going to be far below expectations. Such a rumor could result in a drop in the company's stock price, enabling the agent to purchase shares at an artificially low price. The Uniform Securities Act helps to ensure that persons acting in such an unethical manner can be dealt with appropriately.

PERMITTING CUSTOMERS TO SEEK RESOLUTION TO PROBLEMS

Securities professionals must ensure that any customer-related concerns are handled appropriately and legally. Client complaints must be taken seriously. If a client provides a written complaint to an agent, the agent is obligated to provide the written complaint to their employing broker-dealer. Failure to do so is a violation of the Uniform Securities Act. The Uniform Securities Act also prohibits professionals in the securities industry from trying to get a client to sign a waiver that would prevent the client from entering into litigation in the event the securities professional engages in an illegal activity. In short, persons that are acting as professionals in the securities industry must not act in a manner that is designed to prevent a customer from obtaining resolution to problems or concerns or redress in the event the professional has engaged in prohibited behavior.

ACTING AS PRINCIPAL IN A TRANSACTION

Investment advisers are required to notify their clients any time the investment adviser (or investment adviser representative) is a principal for any recommended security transaction. In other words, the investment adviser must inform their client if the investment adviser actually owns the security it recommends to the client or will buy the security it recommends the client sell. Investment advisers are permitted to act as a principal in this manner; however, the client must be informed prior to the transaction and must acknowledge and approve of the investment adviser's capacity in the transaction in writing prior to the completion of the transaction. This requirement ensures that potential investors are well aware of the investment adviser's potential conflict of interest and helps to prevent unethical investment advisers from using their influence with their clients for their own personal gain.

AGENCY CROSS TRANSACTIONS

In some instances, an investment adviser may act as an adviser and a broker for the same transaction. This activity is referred to as an agency cross transaction. When an investment adviser engages in an agency cross transaction, the investment adviser is compensated for two activities: providing investment advice and acting as a broker for the actual transaction. Because the investment adviser benefits from the transaction itself, the investment adviser must notify its client of the conflict of interest, and the client must provide written consent for the transaction. Although the investment adviser may act as both an adviser and a broker for the transaction, the investment adviser is prohibited from advising both the buyer and the seller in the transaction. The investment adviser must track all agency cross transactions and provide an itemized statement of these transactions on an annual basis.

CLIENT CONFIDENTIALITY

Investment advisers are obligated to protect confidential client information. This means that investment advisers are prohibited from releasing any information regarding their client's identity or the nature of the client's investment. There are only two exceptions to the requirement. First, the client's confidential information may be released if the client authorizes the investment adviser to release the information to a third party. The other exception is if the investment adviser is legally ordered to release the information. This exception normally occurs as the result of a subpoena for information. However, it should be noted that in instances in which the investment adviser is ordered to release the information, the investment adviser must still limit the release to the specific information legally ordered and provide the information only to the party indicated on the subpoena.

EXCESSIVE MARKUP OF A SECURITY

The excessive markup of a security is always a prohibited practice under the Uniform Securities Act; however, an excessive markup of a security is not always considered an act of fraud as well. The excessive markup of a security is considered a fraudulent act only in instances in which the person performing the markup intentionally and attempted to mislead clients regarding the markup. For example, if a broker-dealer informs clients that a security has been marked up by one dollar, and the security has actually been marked up by two dollars, the broker-dealer has committed an act of fraud. Similarly, if a broker-dealer tries to convince its clients that a given markup is standard in the industry for the type of transaction in question, when the broker-dealer knows that the markup is excessive, the broker-dealer has committed fraud.

FRAUD REGARDING FALSE OR MISLEADING STATEMENTS

Fraud only occurs when a person intentionally attempts to mislead. If a person misquotes a market price to a client due to the transposition of a number, a computer glitch or other error, the person has not committed fraud. If a person fails to provide a material fact to a client because the person was unaware of the fact, or because the person did not realize that the fact in question might influence the client's investment decision, the person has not committed fraud. While these instances are not considered fraud, it is important to keep in mind that a securities professional is obligated to safeguard against this type of error. Furthermore, in all of the instances listed above, if the securities professional later became aware that a mistake had been made, failure to disclose the error to the client would be an act of fraud.

SEGREGATATION OF CLIENT ACCOUNTS

The ethical management of all client accounts is a vital part of a broker-dealer's responsibilities. A broker-dealer must segregate client accounts appropriately. Broker-dealers may not place securities that are owned by a client in the firm's own account. Instead, client-owned securities must be placed in a separate client account. Broker-dealers must also segregate any free securities belonging to a client. Free securities are any securities in a margin account that are not collateral for the margin loan. These requirements have been instituted to help ensure that broker-dealers maintain client accounts in an ethical manner. A broker-dealer's failure to properly segregate client accounts may result in the denial, suspension, or revocation of the broker-dealer's license.

RESPONSIBILITY TO MAKE AVAILABLE SECURITIES THAT ARE ALLOTTED FOR DISTRIBUTION

If a broker-dealer is allotted a specific quantity of a security for distribution, the broker-dealer must make the entire allotment available under a bona fide public offering. This requirement applies whether the broker-dealer is itself an underwriter or a member of the selling group, or if the broker-dealer has merely acquired the security from another party that is an underwriter or member of the selling group for distribution. In any of these instances, the broker-dealer may not withhold distribution of a security that it has been entrusted to distribute. For example, a broker-dealer that has been granted a specific allotment of securities for an IPO offering cannot hold onto some of those securities while waiting to see how high the price will climb. Instead, the broker-dealer must offer all of the securities that it has been allotted.

DISCLOSURE OF RELATIONSHIPS BETWEEN BROKER-DEALER AND ISSUER OF A SECURITY

Broker-dealers must ensure that clients are informed of certain relationships between the broker-dealer and the issuer of a security. If a broker-dealer controls the issuer of a security, is controlled by the issuer of a security, is affiliated with the issuer of a security, or is controlled by an entity that also controls the issuer of a security, the broker-dealer must disclose this information to its clients prior to initiating any sale or purchase of the security on behalf of the client. The initial disclosure may be made verbally. However, if the initial disclosure is made verbally, a written disclosure must follow and must be provided to the client by the time the security transaction is complete. A broker-dealer that fails to comply with this requirement may face the denial, suspension, or revocation of its registration.

PROPER BORROWING AND LENDING PRACTICES

Agents must ensure that they maintain a proper relationship with their customers. To that end, agents must not borrow money or securities from their customers or lend money or securities to their customers. In addition, an agent should not allow customers to leave funds or securities in the agent's care. In short, an agent should not perform the functions of borrowing, lending, and protecting a client's funds or securities. Agents should make recommendations to their clients regarding possible

84

securities transactions. Agents must guard against any improper financial dealings with customers. Inappropriate borrowing or lending of funds or securities between customers and agents can result in the agent's loss of registration. Similarly, the registration of agent that inappropriately takes custody of a customer's funds or securities may be suspended, revoked, or denied.

REFRAINING FROM SUGGESTIONS OF EXCESSIVE TRADING

Investment advisers must not attempt to persuade their clients to engage in trading practices that are unnecessarily large or frequent. This prohibition applies whether an investment adviser is making trade recommendation to its client or is actually using the discretionary power granted by the client to make trades. This provision helps to ensure that investment advisers act as responsible fiduciaries. Depending upon an individual investment adviser's circumstances, an investment adviser may have a direct or indirect financial incentive to increase the client's volume of trades. For example, some investment advisers may receive compensation from a broker-dealer for each trade. It would be highly unethical for an investment adviser to recommend frequent trading to a client in order to increase the investment adviser's compensation from a broker-dealer. Instead, investment advisers are obligated to ensure that each and every trade is recommended based solely on the best interests of the client.

DISCLOSURE OF POTENTIAL CONFLICT-OF-INTEREST SITUATIONS

Investment advisers must provide written notification to their clients of any material conflict of interest that the investment adviser or any of its employees have that could hinder the investment adviser's ability to provide objective and unbiased investment advice. For example, if the investment adviser (or any of the investment adviser's employees) may receive compensation from a source other than the client's fees (for example, from a broker-dealer) for activities associated with the client's investments or securities transactions, the investment adviser must notify the client of this fact in writing. Similarly, investment advisers must also provide written notification if the investment adviser (or its employees) receive commission for transactions in addition to the investment adviser's advisory fee. Investment advisers must provide the written notification of the conflict of interest to their client or clients before providing any investment advice related to the conflict of interest.

USE OF THIRD PARTIES TO PERFORM PROHIBITED PRACTICES

Investment advisers are prohibited from utilizing third parties, whether directly or indirectly, to engage in behavior that would otherwise be prohibited for the investment adviser. In other words, investment advisers cannot attempt to bypass an obligation by having a third party do something on their behalf. For example, investment advisers are prohibited from providing inaccurate or misleading information to their clients or potential clients regarding their qualifications. Since investment advisers are prohibited from engaging in this type of behavior, investment advisers are also prohibited from asking a third party to pass along false or misleading information regarding the investment adviser's qualifications to clients or potential clients. If an investment adviser is prohibited from engaging in a particular behavior, the investment adviser is also prohibited from having a third party engage in the prohibited behavior on their behalf.

UNIFORM SECURITIES ACT'S PROVISIONS REGARDING ETHICAL BUSINESS PRACTICES

Although the Uniform Securities Act specifies many required business practices and prohibited business practices for broker-dealers, agents, investment advisers, and investment adviser representatives, the listed business practices are not intended to be all-inclusive. Rather, the listed business practices are merely provided as examples of specific scenarios that have already been evaluated and ruled upon. To the extent a specific business practice has already been addressed, securities professionals must comply with the provisions already established. In instances where a specific business practice has not been specifically addressed, securities professionals are required to use good judgment and act ethically at all times. Regardless of whether a particular practice has been previously examined, all persons acting as broker-dealers, agents, investment advisers, and investment advisers representatives are required to follow sound and ethical business practices at all times.

PROHIBITED BUSINESS PRACTICE AND FRAUDULENT BUSINESS PRACTICE

Under the provisions of the Uniform Securities Act, all fraudulent business practices are prohibited; however, not all prohibited business practices are considered fraudulent. A fraudulent business practice occurs in instances where a person intentionally acts in a deceptive or misleading manner. Such actions are prohibited. However, fraudulent business practices are not the only business practices prohibited by the Uniform Securities Act. The Uniform Securities Act prohibits persons engaged in securities transactions from conducting themselves unethically, even if the unethical behavior does not involve any attempt to deceive. The provisions of the Uniform Securities Act protect the public from unethical business practices of all types; however, fraudulent behavior may result in more severe penalties than other types of unethical behavior.

INSIDER TRADING

The term "insider trading" refers to an individual with "inside" knowledge of a publicly traded company capitalizing on the knowledge to make money. The only instance in which this is legal is when the knowledge that the insider has is publicly available. The term "insider" generally refers to officers, directors, and board members of publicly traded companies, but the term may be applied to any person who may be privy to non-public information, such as the spouse of a director, or a custodial employee who has overheard the non-public information. Depending on the severity of the insider-trading charge, a conviction of insider trading can carry felony prison terms for perpetrators. Additionally, inside traders can be compelled to pay up to three times the amount of money made or three times the amount of loss avoided associated with their inside trading transaction.

SELLING AWAY

Selling away refers to registered individuals making securities transactions somewhere other than the broker-dealer with which they have agency. It is sometimes referred to as "selling off the books." In short, securities transactions by agents must be recorded in their broker-dealer's records. Selling away is generally a prohibited practice, as it may breach their contract with their current broker-dealer and assist with a registered individual's attempt to transact fraudulently. The term "selling away" covers all securities transactions, and exceptions are not made for private offerings and personal transactions. For registered individuals to execute a legal sold-away transaction, they must obtain express permission in writing from the broker-dealer that they currently represent.

CLIENT'S RIGHTS OF RECOVERY

If an advisor gives advice that violates the Uniform Securities Act (USA), the client purchasing the advice may request that the Administrator investigate the occurrence. If the Administrator agrees with the client, he or she may order that the client be refunded the cost of the advice, any losses associated with the advice, a fair interest rate (to be set by the Administrator) on the initial investment , and any legal or court costs associated with the claim (within reason). It is important to note that only when improper securities are sold may the purchaser recover the purchase price. If improper advice is given, the purchaser may only recover the cost of the advice plus any losses incurred due to the advice, but not the original principal.

CYBERSECURITY

Investment advisers have strong fiduciary duties to protect the sensitive customer information and data which they hold in custody. In our age of increasingly complex and elaborate technology, this duty naturally extends to considerations of cybersecurity. Accordingly investment advisers ought to implement best practices concerning cybersecurity, which can include but is not limited to the following:

- preventing, identifying, and alleviating identity theft
- storing electronic data such that they cannot be rewritten or erased
- adopting policies, procedures, and training pertaining to cybersecurity
- utilizing encrypted or secure servers, emails, and other media as necessary or feasible
- installing antivirus software
- enacting confidentiality agreements with third-party service providers

Test Strategies

DOUBLE NEGATIVES IN TEST QUESTIONS

The wording of some of the test questions may be tricky. For example, the Uniform Securities Act declares that certain actions are unlawful. This simply means that such activities are illegal. If the test asks about activities that are "not unlawful," remember the rule of double negatives. Two negative statements (like "not" and "unlawful") cancel each other out and make a positive statement. If an action is not unlawful, then it is lawful (or legal). A test question that asks which of the following activities is "not unlawful" is simply asking which of the following activities is legal. Another example of a double negative statement that may appear on the test would be a question that begins "None of the following actions are prohibited except...." A question that begins in this manner is asking which of the actions listed below are permitted under the Uniform Securities Act.

BASIC TEST-TAKING STRATEGIES FOR THE SERIES 63 EXAM

Many of the questions on the Series 63 exam are detailed and complex. In order to answer these questions correctly, it is important to read each question slowly and thoroughly. Each aspect of the question must be taken into consideration when determining the correct response. Make note of the people the question references. The answer may be different for a broker-dealer than for an investment adviser representative. Determine whether the question is asking for the response that fits the described scenario or the response that does not fit the described scenario. Recognize any specific locations identified in the question. Activities that occur in one location may require a different response that activities that occur in another location.

TEST QUESTIONS COMBINING DOUBLE NEGATIVE STATEMENTS WITH REQUESTS TO IDENTIFY EXCEPTIONS

Questions on the test may combine a double negative statement with the instruction to identify an exception. For example, a question may state, "The following business practices are not unlawful except..." It is important to review the question in its entirety. In this example, the first part of the question reads, "The following business practices are not unlawful." That part of the question can be read to mean, "The following business practices are lawful." The second part of the question is the "except." This means that the correct response is the item (or items) that does not fit in the identified scenario (legal business practices). In this case, the question could be reworded as "Which of the following business practices is illegal?"

TEST QUESTIONS ASKING FOR IDENTIFICATION OF EXCEPTIONS

Many of the questions on the test are worded in this manner: "All of the following _____ are _____ except..." When this type of question appears, the question is simply asking you to identify the items listed below that do not fit into the identified scenarios. For example, the test might state, "All of the following items are considered securities except..." For this question, the correct answer would identify

88

all of the responses that are not securities. It is important to read the question carefully as a single word can change the entire meaning of the question. For example, if the question above were changed to read, "None of the following items are considered securities except…" the correct answer would identify the items that are securities.

ANSWERING TEST QUESTIONS THAT ASK WHICH RESPONSE IS CONSISTENT WITH A SPECIFIED SCENARIO

Some test questions may ask which of the responses meets a specific condition. These questions may be worded in this manner: "In which of the following cases did _____." When responding to these questions, it is important to fully understand all aspects of the identified condition. For example, if the question asks "In which of the following cases did an agent make a lawful offer of sale?" each piece of the condition (an agent made a lawful offer of sale) must be considered. The correct response will reflect all of the pieces of the condition. In this example, the correct response must include an agent and a lawful offer of sale. Incorrect responses could include a lawful offer of sale made by a broker-dealer, an unlawful offer of sale made by an agent, or a lawful offer to buy made by an agent.

RESPONDING TO COMPLEX TEST QUESTIONS

Some of the questions on the test are complex. For example, a question might pose a scenario in which an agent was aware of certain facts and then behaved in a certain manner. The question would then ask if the agent's actions are appropriate. Before answering the question, it is important to break the question down into its components. For example, if the scenario involves an agent, the correct response will relate to the responsibilities of an agent, not to the responsibilities of an investment adviser. If the question notes that the agent is aware of certain facts, then the correct response must consider how knowledge of those facts impacts (or should have impacted) the agent's actions.

QUESTIONS WITH COMBINATIONS OF RESPONSES THAT COMPLY WITH A PARTICULAR SCENARIO

The questions on the exam are multiple-choice questions. In some instances, the test will identify four possible responses to the question and then ask the test taker to identify the combination of the responses that are correct. When answering this type of question, all of the correct responses must be included in the answer. For example, if both the first and last responses fit the identified scenario, an answer that only identifies the first response would be incorrect. Similarly, if the second response does not fit in the identified scenario, no answer that includes the second response can be correct. With this type of question, if the test taker knows that one of the responses does fit the identified scenarios and another does not, the test taker may be able to arrive at the correct answer through the process of elimination even if the test taker is uncertain about the other responses.

Series 63 Practice Test

Want to take this practice test in an online interactive format? Check out the bonus page, which includes interactive practice questions and much more: **mometrix.com/bonus948/series63**

1. Which federal legislation do individual states use to establish uniform and understandable securities laws across the United States?
   a. The Securities Act of 1933
   b. The Securities Exchange Act of 1934
   c. The Uniform Securities Act
   d. Federal Blue Sky laws

2. Which type of transaction is not covered under the anti-fraud provisions of the Uniform Securities Act?
   a. A completed sale of a security
   b. A contract agreeing to a sale
   c. A direct offer to sell a security at a stated price
   d. A solicitation of an offer to sell

3. Which Act established a division of responsibility between state and federal regulators?
   a. National Securities Markets Improvements Act of 1996
   b. Uniform Securities Act
   c. Gramm-Rudman Act
   d. Securities Investor Protection Act of 1970

4. Which Act establishes special requirements for publicly issued debt securities in excess of $5,000,000 during a 12-month period?
   a. Public Utility Holding Company Act of 1935
   b. Trust Indenture Act of 1939
   c. Securities Investor Protection Act of 1970
   d. Bank Secrecy Act

5. The Gramm-Leach Bliley Act protects investors by requiring investment advisors to...
   a. provide full disclosure
   b. be registered with the SEC
   c. establish safeguards to protect clients' non-public information
   d. establish standards for managing client funds

6. Which definition of a "person" is used by the Uniform Securities Act?

a. Legal person
b. Natural person
c. An individual
d. None of the above

7. Which type of person must be registered under the Uniform Securities Act?

a. Broker-dealer
b. Registered representative
c. Securities analyst
d. Employees of a broker-dealer

8. The Uniform Securities Act defines which of the following as an investment adviser?

a. Investment adviser representative
b. Federally covered investment adviser
c. Broker-dealer
d. Financial planner

9. Under the Uniform Securities Act, a person is considered an investment adviser if...

a. as an incidental part of business, he receives compensation for securities advice
b. as a regular course of business, he provides securities advice to unrelated persons
c. as a regular course of business, he receives compensation for securities advice
d. as an incidental part of business, he provides securities advice to unrelated persons

10. Which title defines a person associated with an investment adviser who manages accounts or portfolios?

a. Account representative
b. Investment adviser representative
c. Federally covered investment adviser
d. Administrative assistant

11. An investment adviser would not be required to register in a state where it conducts business if...

a. the investment adviser's clients are institutional investors
b. the investment adviser's clients travel outside of the state
c. an investment adviser's existing client relocates to another state
d. None of the above

12. Which is not an example of an exempt security?

  a. Municipal securities
  b. Securities for trust companies
  c. Investment contracts for employee stock purchases
  d. Private placements of securities

13. Which regulatory agency determines which information is required of the investment adviser for registration?

  a. The state's Administrator
  b. The Securities and Exchange Commission
  c. FINRA
  d. The state securities commissioner

14. The maximum amount the state Administrator may require for a surety bond for an investment adviser, or broker-dealer that has discretionary authority over clients' funds is...

  a. $5,000
  b. $10,000
  c. $35,000
  d. $50,000

15. When reviewing the qualifications of a firm seeking licensing as a broker-dealer or investment adviser, which of the firm's personnel can an Administrator consider in the registration review process?

  a. The personnel or associates involved in activities involving securities
  b. Clerical personnel that provide support to investment advisers
  c. Persons who have invested in the firm but are not involved in the day-to-day activities
  d. All of the above

16. How long must investment advisers and broker-dealers keep required records available for review?

  a. Three years for investment advisers and five years for broker-dealers
  b. Three years for both investment advisers and broker-dealers
  c. Three years for broker-dealers and five years for investment advisers
  d. Five years for both investment advisers and broker-dealers

17. A condition mandatory for the existence of a common enterprise is...

  a. profits are distributed to the investor on an annual basis
  b. profits and losses of the investor are tied to the profits and losses of other investors
  c. an investment contract
  d. the investor having at least a 5% interest in the common enterprise

18. Under the Uniform Securities Act, which is not considered a security?

    a. Commodities traded on a futures market
    b. An investment contract
    c. Treasury stock
    d. Certificate of interest

19. Which documents do Administrators review when evaluating the registration statement for a security?

    a. The preliminary prospectus
    b. The issuer's financial statements
    c. The issuer's business plan
    d. The proposed promotional materials

20. If a state Administrator plans to revoke the registration of a security, what must be provided to the issuer of that security?

    a. A cease-and-desist order
    b. A temporary suspension pending the outcome of a hearing
    c. A written findings of fact and conclusions of law
    d. A notice of a hearing

21. Which information is included in a prospectus, but not in a preliminary prospectus?

    a. The offering price of the security and the name of the underwriter
    b. The offering price of the security and the date the security is available
    c. The name of the underwriter and the date the security is available
    d. The date the security is available and a statement that the securities have been reviewed by the state Administrator

22. Registration by Coordination refers to a procedure that reduces the duplication of effort between...

    a. multiple underwriters of a single security
    b. the issuer and underwriter of a security
    c. state and federal securities regulators
    d. the SEC and FINRA

23. What pre-requisite must an issuer meet to qualify for the Registration by Notice filing method?

    a. In business for a minimum of five years
    b. Register the security with the SEC prior to registration with the state
    c. Net worth of at least $500,000
    d. In business for a minimum of three years

24. Under which registration method does a registration for securities become effective at 3 pm Eastern Standard Time on the second business day after the request for registration is filed?

a. Registration by Filing process
b. Registration by Qualification
c. Registration by Notice filing
d. Registration by Coordination

25. Under the Registration by Qualification process, which information about the issuer of a security is not required?

a. The issuer's name and address
b. The business structure of the issuer
c. A list of the issuer's competitors
d. Equipment owned by the issuer

26. Under the anti-fraud provisions of the Uniform Securities Act, a state Administrator can enforce securities fraud for which of the following types of securities registrations?

a. Securities registered with the state
b. A federally covered security
c. A security that does not have to be registered with the SEC or the state Administrator
d. All of the above

27. Which securities are not exempt from registration with the state Administrator?

a. Securities guaranteed by an insurance company to finance a debt
b. Securities governed by the Public Utility Holding Company Act
c. Securities issued as a private placement
d. Federally covered securities

28. The federal Act that prohibits state Administrators from regulating securities already under the Securities And Exchange Commission regulatory purview is...

a. The Uniform Securities Act
b. The Securities Exchange Act of 1934
c. The National Securities Markets Improvement Act of 1996
d. The Securities Act of 1933

29. According to the Uniform Securities Act, what constitutes a fraudulent business practice?

a. A person intentionally acting in an unethical manner
b. A person intentionally acting in a deceptive or misleading manner
c. Investment advice that leads to a loss in a client's account
d. Investment performance being inconsistent with the expectations provided by the investment advisor

94

30. What is the definition of a material fact?

a. Information provided by the Board of Directors of an issuer of a security
b. Information found in the financial statements of an investment
c. Information found in the prospectus for a security
d. Information that an investor relies upon when deciding whether or not to invest

31. Which is considered a fraudulent act?

a. Agreeing to perform services for clients that the broker-dealer is not qualified to perform
b. Failing to provide information to a client that could impact the client's investment decision
c. Not disclosing that transaction charges are built into the transaction as a markup
d. All of the above

32. How does the Uniform Securities Act define inside information?

a. Facts that have not been made public that could impact the value of a security
b. Client account information that a securities professional must maintain
c. Information a securities professional delivers to a client to enable him to make an investment decision
d. Information provided to a client regarding an upcoming change in listing for a security

33. Under what conditions may a securities professional borrow funds or securities from a client?

a. When the client is a family member
b. If the client initiated the transaction
c. When the client offers securities loans as a regular part of business
d. Under no conditions

34. Which activity is prohibited when recording transactions in a client's account?

a. Not recording a transaction at the request of the client
b. Confirming the client's order specifications over the Internet
c. Backdating a record to correct an error in the original transaction
d. All of the above

35. The excessive markup of a security is not considered an act of fraud when...

a. the broker-dealer informs clients of an incorrect markup
b. the quoted markup is represented as an industry standard
c. the markup was a clerical error
d. the broker-dealer knows the markup is excessive

36. Under the Uniform Securities Act, which type of guarantee is prohibited?

    a. A guarantee that has been verified by a third party

    b. A recommendation based on prior year financial statements

    c. A guarantee based on the prospectus

    d. A guarantee of future performance of a security's principal return, dividends or interest

37. What occurs when parties engage in matching purchases?

    a. A significant increase in outstanding shares

    b. An artificial increase in the market value of a security

    c. Small shareholders realize capital losses

    d. The parties pay a lower commission

38. In addition to client authorization, what else must a securities professional obtain when establishing a margin account for a client?

    a. A margin signature card

    b. A written margin agreement

    c. A verbal margin agreement

    d. Written client authorization

39. Segregating client accounts is a practice wherein...

    a. each account may only contain the funds belonging to one client

    b. client funds must be deposited with a financial institution not affiliated with the broker-dealer

    c. broker-dealer funds must be held by a custodian

    d. client-owned securities may not be placed in the broker-dealer's account

40. A broker-dealer participating in a public offering must make available what percentage of its allotment?

    a. 75%

    b. 80%

    c. 90%

    d. 100%

41. Under what circumstances may a registered agent represent multiple registered broker-dealers?

    a. With written permission from the broker-dealers

    b. When the broker-dealers are affiliated with each other

    c. With written permission from the SEC

    d. With written permission from FINRA

42. Before recommending investments, a securities professional must obtain and consider client information integral to determining...

    a. the client's investment goals
    b. the client's risk tolerance
    c. the amount of investment the client can afford
    d. the client's financial position

43. Which information is used when making an investment recommendation?

    a. A rumor the investment adviser has reason to believe is true
    b. Company marketing literature
    c. Verifiable facts
    d. All of the above

44. Under what circumstances can an investment adviser share in a client's profits or losses?

    a. The client has provided written approval
    b. The agent has a joint account with the client
    c. The agent holds over 50% share in the client's account
    d. An agent cannot share profits or losses with clients

45. When may an investment adviser release information about a client's investments?

    a. When the adviser releases information to companies in which the client has invested
    b. When the information pertains to the client's investment portfolio
    c. When directed by the broker-dealer where the adviser is licensed
    d. When the investment adviser is legally ordered to release the information

46. What must an investment adviser do when a material conflict of interest impairs its ability to provide objective investment advice?

    a. Transfer the client's account to a different investment adviser
    b. Provide written notification to the client
    c. Remove the source of the conflict of interest
    d. Inform the broker-dealer of the conflict of interest

47. Under what condition can an investment adviser maintain custody of a client's assets?

    a. If it is the policy of the broker-dealer
    b. Under written permission from the client
    c. Under written permission from the Administrator
    d. When the Administrator has not ruled to prohibit custody

48. Which other role of an investment adviser would make it permissible to loan money to a client?

    a. The investment adviser is a family member of the client
    b. The investment adviser is a financial institution
    c. The investment adviser is a broker-dealer
    d. An investment adviser is prohibited from loaning money to all clients

49. In their roles as fiduciaries, investment advisers...

    a. must provide clients with sound investment recommendations
    b. cannot promote their own interests above the interests of their clients
    c. can execute transactions for clients
    d. cannot make unsolicited investment recommendations

50. How often must an investment adviser obtain client authorization for securities transactions?

    a. Before the first transaction if the client has provided written authorization
    b. Before receiving instructions from a third party
    c. Before every transaction
    d. When creating an annual financial plan

51. Which information is not permissible content in an investment adviser's advertising materials?

    a. Information regarding the historical performance of a security
    b. Information regarding the performance of recommendations
    c. Historical security prices
    d. Testimonials

52. What information must an investment adviser disclose to a client when using a report that was prepared by another party?

    a. The date of the report
    b. The name of the third party
    c. Recommendations that are based on the report
    d. Performance of the recommendations based on the report

53. Under what circumstance is a state Administrator's authority not limited to its individual state of jurisdiction?

    a. During a SEC investigation
    b. To help enforce an out of state subpoena
    c. When prosecuting a complaint
    d. An Administrator's authority is limited to a single state

54. How does an Administrator prevent an anticipated violation of the Uniform Securities Act?

    a. By holding a hearing
    b. By issuing an injunction
    c. By issuing a cease-and-desist order
    d. By issuing a subpoena

55. Which condition must exist for an Administrator to have jurisdiction over a securities transaction?

    a. The transaction must originate within the Administrator's state
    b. The transaction must be directed to the Administrator's state
    c. The transaction must be accepted in the Administrator's state
    d. Any of the above

56. Which is not considered a security sale?

    a. A security is transferred for an item of value
    b. One party extends an offer to transfer ownership of the security for an item of value
    c. A party offers a security as an incentive to sell a non-security
    d. A party pays for services with a security

57. A state Administrator ensures that investors are protected by...

    a. issuing orders
    b. assessing penalties
    c. levying fines
    d. imposing criminal penalties

58. What action may a state Administrator take if an applicant does not meet the minimum required financial standards?

    a. Deny the applicant's registration
    b. Suspend the applicant's registration
    c. Revoke an applicant's registration
    d. Any of the above

59. A state Administrator may cancel a registration when...

    a. the registrant has committed a fraud
    b. the registrant has manipulated a customer's account
    c. the registrant has churned a customer's account
    d. the registrant is no longer considered a legal person

60. Which is critical when proving fraud in a securities transaction?

    a. Misleading information must have been provided
    b. A recommendation based on false information must have been made
    c. A person withheld information from a client
    d. A person must deliberately act in a manner designed to mislead

Answer Key and Explanations

1. C: The Uniform Securities Act. The Uniform Securities Act (USA) provides consistent regulation across all states, protects investors and promotes public interests. The Act governs securities transactions, and individuals and firms that conduct securities transactions or provide security-related investment advice. The Act sets guidelines for individual states to enact their own securities laws, which are commonly known as Blue Sky laws. First introduced in 1930, most states did not adopt the Act's guidelines until its major revision in 1956. The Act was revised in 1985 and 1988, but most states still use the 1956 guidelines. A 2002 update has been used as framework in just a dozen states. In addition, the USA defines the characteristics of the individuals and entities that are subject to regulation under the Act. The USA is applicable in any jurisdiction where it has been adopted as legislation.

2. D: A solicitation of an offer to sell. The anti-fraud provisions of the Uniform Securities Act (USA) apply to all offers and sales of securities. An offer is an attempt to make a security available to another party and includes completed sales, sales contracts and direct offers where one person is willing to sell (or otherwise dispose of) a security at a given price. The USA provisions also apply to indirect offers (the solicitation of an offer to buy), where the offer is made by a person who is not the owner of the particular security for sale. The USA defines the terms "sale" and "offer" broadly, helping to protect potential investors against the possibility that a transaction would be structured in such a way that might fall outside of a narrower definition of a sale, an offer or a purchase in order to not be subject to anti-fraud provisions.

3. A: National Securities Markets Improvements Act of 1996. The National Securities Markets Improvements Act of 1996 (NSMIA) established a division of responsibility between state regulators and federal regulators. The NSMIA eliminates the duplication of efforts between federal and state governments by defining the specific securities and transactions that fall under federal jurisdiction. NSMIA regulates certain investment advisers, with ones falling under the Securities And Exchange Commission (SEC) jurisdiction considered federally covered advisers, and not subject to investor adviser regulation by the Uniform Securities Act. Securities covered under NSMIA include:

- Nationally traded securities, such as those listed or authorized for listing on NYSE or NASDAQ
- Registered investment company securities
- Offers and sales of exempt securities
- Securities offered pursuant to SEC Rule 506

4. B: Trust Indenture Act of 1939. The Trust Indenture Act of 1939 requires that public debt (bonds, notes and debentures) issues of $5,000,000 or more be placed

100

under the supervision of a "suitably independent and qualified trustee" to ensure that bondholders' rights are not compromised. It also requires that the particulars of the issue are fully disclosed. The Public Utility Holding Company Act of 1935, a consumer protection Act guarding against abuse, requires holding companies for gas and electric utilities be federally registered, unless exempt from registration. The Securities Investor Protection Act of 1970 established the Securities Investor Protection Corporation (SIPC), a federally mandated insurance company that insures the investors up to $500,000 if a broker-dealer defaults, goes bankrupt or commits fraud. The Bank Secrecy Act (BSA), also referred to as the Currency and Foreign Transactions Reporting Act, is federal legislation targeting financial institutions that may be aiding clients attempting to launder money, evade taxes or engage in other criminal behavior.

5. C: Establish safeguards to protect clients' non-public information. The Gramm-Leach Bliley Act, or SEC Regulation S-P, created regulations to protect the private information of investors. The Act requires investment companies, investment advisers, broker-dealers and financial institutions to protect clients' confidential information by:

- Establishing safeguards to protect their clients' non-public information from inadvertent disclosure
- Establishing processes that ensure the safe disposal of client credit information
- Providing written notice of the practices used to protect client confidentiality
- Prohibiting the disclosure of a client's non-public information to non-affiliated third parties without the client's consent

6. A: Legal person. The Uniform Securities Act defines a "person" as an individual, corporation, business trust, estate, trust, partnership, limited liability company (LLC), association, joint venture, government, governmental agency, public corporation, or any legal or commercial entity. A legal person can or may:

- Enter into contracts with other legal persons
- Engage in business transactions
- Be charged with and found guilty of criminal activity
- Be sued and may face civil litigation
- Be required to pay damages if found to be at fault in a civil suit

7. A: Broker-dealer. The Uniform Securities Act (USA) requires broker-dealers, agents, investment advisers, or investment adviser representatives be registered with their state's Administrator. Broker-dealers and investment advisers may be individuals or companies. Agents and investment adviser representatives are always individuals. Persons acting in any of these four capacities must apply for, obtain and maintain registration, ensuring they are qualified to act in those capacities. The USA regulates persons acting in any of these four capacities and the state Administrator oversees their activities.

8. D: Financial planner. Under the Uniform Securities Act, an investment adviser is defined as someone who:

- Receives compensation for advising others, either directly or through publications, about the value of securities or the advisability of trading securities
- Provides, as part of a regular business, analyses or reports concerning securities

Investment advisers receive flat fees, or fees based on a percentage of managed assets. Under the Act, the following are excluded from the definition of investment adviser:

- An investment adviser representative
- A lawyer, accountant, engineer or teacher who provides investment advice as an incidental practice of the person's profession
- A broker-dealer who provides investment advice in the normal course of business and does not receive special compensation for the investment advice
- A publisher of a newspaper, news magazine or financial publication
- A federally-covered investment adviser
- A bank or savings institution
- A person excluded by the Investment Advisers Act of 1940

9. C: As a regular course of business, he receives compensation for securities advice. The Uniform Securities Act specifies three requirements for being considered an investment adviser:

- The person must offer advice to others concerning securities; this may be recommendations regarding the purchase and/or sale of securities, or an evaluation of the value of specific securities
- The advice offered must be part of the person's continuing line of business
- The person offering the advice must receive compensation for the investment advice

10. B: Investment adviser representative. An investment adviser representative is an individual employed by, or associated with, an investment adviser, or federally covered investment adviser, and who:

- Makes recommendations or gives investment advice regarding securities
- Manages accounts or portfolios of clients
- Determines which recommendation or advice regarding securities should be given
- Provides investment advice
- Receives compensation to solicit, offer, or negotiate the sale of, or for selling investment advice
- Supervises employees who perform any of these activities

102

11. A: The investment adviser's clients are institutional investors. Investment advisers must register with the SEC, or within each state in which they conduct business. An investment adviser is exempt from registration in a particular state (State A) when it does not have a place of business within that state and is already registered in another state (State B). This exception, however, depends on the number and type of clients the investment adviser serves in State A; if its only clients in State A are registered broker-dealers, other investment advisers, institutional investors or persons with a primary residence in State B, the investment adviser is not required to register in State A. Also, an investment adviser with five or fewer clients (other than the aforementioned types) in State A that is already registered in State B, is not obligated to register in State A to conduct business.

12. D: Private placements of securities. An exempt security is one that does not require registration. If an issuer deals only with exempt securities, the representatives of that agency are not considered agents from a regulatory perspective. Provided there's no compensation associated with the transaction, those representatives do not need to register as agents with a state Administrator, However, if an issuer has both exempt and registered securities, any representatives of that issuer who deal with the registered securities must be registered agents. A variety of securities are considered exempt, including:

- Federal and municipal securities
- Securities for domestic banks, savings and loan institutions, and trust companies
- Securities underlying investment contracts for employee investments such as pension plans and employee stock purchases

13. A: The state's Administrator. The state's Administrator decides which information is required for registration of an investment adviser, with such information focused on the individual or individuals seeking registration, the services to be offered, the proposed business location, the legal structure of the firm, and its financial soundness. For broker-dealers and investment advisers, this information may be required for any and all partners, associates, or directors. Required information may include:

- The type and location of the desired business
- The investment adviser's proposed means of doing business
- Current qualifications
- Performance history
- Negative rulings, both civil and criminal, relating to securities
- Financial history

14. B: $10,000. A surety bond of $10,000 is normally required in cases where a client grants discretionary authority to an investment adviser for the purpose of managing his account(s). The state's Administrator may establish minimum financial standards for investment advisers, and if it determines a surety bond or other form of security is required, the maximum amount permitted under federal regulations is $10,000. Other surety bond amounts would correspond to the amount of authority the investment adviser would have over client funds. For example, if the investment adviser maintains custody of client accounts, a bond of $35,000 is normally required. The deposit for the surety bonds may be made by cash or securities. If securities are used to secure the surety bond, the Administrator may specify the type of security that may be used. In addition, broker-dealers and investment advisers may be required to meet minimum net capital requirements.

15. A: The personnel or associates involved in activities involving securities. When an Administrator reviews the qualifications of a firm seeking licensing as a broker-dealer or investment adviser, only personnel or associates that are actively involved in securities activities may be considered. While an Administrator may review the firm, its agents and investment adviser representatives, it must exclude from consideration the personnel that work for the firm, or people invested in the firm, who are not involved in day-to-day securities activities. Furthermore, the Administrator may not review the firm's maintenance or clerical staffs, as they do not perform securities transactions. Finally, an Administrator may not deny a license based on the applicant's lack of experience as long as the applicant has demonstrated qualification based on training or knowledge.

16. C: Three years for broker-dealers and five years for investment advisers. The Uniform Securities Act (USA) gives a state Administrator the authority to review the business records belonging to broker-dealers and investment advisers. These records include, but are not limited to, account records, papers and correspondence. Broker-dealers must keep them for three years, while investment advisers have that responsibility for five years. Non-compliance with a records request made by a state Administrator is a violation of the USA.

17. B: Profits and losses of the investor are tied to the profits and losses of other investors. Common enterprises are one of the forms of an investment contract, therefore they are securities. In a common enterprise, the profits and losses of the investor are tied to the profits and losses of other investors, the party offering the investment or a third party. The "fortune" of the investor is dependent upon the success and work of others. Another example of an investment contract is an investment providing interest in a limited partnership.

18. A: Commodities traded on a futures market. The Uniform Securities Act (USA) defines a security as a note, stock, treasury stock, security future, bond, debenture, evidence of indebtedness, certificate of interest or participation in a profit-sharing agreement, collateral trust certificate, pre-organization certificate or subscription, transferable share, investment contract, voting trust certificate or certificate of deposit for a security. The USA does not regulate transactions that do not involve securities. Investment options offered by banks, such as certificates of deposit (CDs) insured by the FDIC, are not securities. Insurance companies also offer a number of investment options that are not considered securities, including fixed annuity offerings and various forms of life insurance. Commodities that trade on a futures market are also excluded from the definition of securities.

19. D: The proposed promotional materials. Administrators review an issuer's proposed promotional materials by virtue of the fact that it must review the registration statement for a security prior to allowing it to be registered in the state. This review helps the Administrator ensure that the offering will be presented appropriately and that the promotional materials are not misleading or unethical in any material respect. Also considered are any pertinent facts related to the registration and the offering of the security in other jurisdictions. The Administrator also evaluates the contractual relationship between the issuer and the underwriters, as well as agreements between the underwriters.

20. C: A written findings of fact and conclusions of law. A state Administrator planning to issue an order to deny, suspend or revoke the registration of a security must first provide notice of its intent and a written findings of fact and conclusions of law to the security's issuer. Upon receipt of these items, the issuer has the right to contest the findings by requesting a hearing. Although an Administrator cannot issue its order without providing advanced notice, it may exercise its right to issue an emergency cease-and-desist order if the situation warrants such treatment. If necessary, the Administrator also has the ability to issue a type of temporary suspension pending the outcome of the hearing. These provisions help ensure that the issuer receives fair treatment while the Administrator works to protect investors.

21. B: The offering price of the security and the date the security is available. The preliminary prospectus contains the same information as the prospectus except for the offering price and the date the security is available. It's referred to as a "red herring" because it contains a notification in the document, in red, that the document is not an attempt to sell the security. During the period following registration of the security with the Securities and Exchange Commission but before the security is initially sold, broker-dealers may send the preliminary prospectus to prospective investors who have indicated an interest in possibly buying the security. A preliminary prospectus provides potential investors with the information necessary to analyze the potential investment in advance of the offering.

22. C: State and federal securities regulators. Registration by Coordination is designed to minimize the unnecessary duplication of effort between state and federal securities regulators. The process is used when a security must be registered with the Securities And Exchange Commission (SEC) because it is an interstate offering (an offering that will be made available in more than one state) but the issuer is not large enough to be exempt from state registration. Using this process, each of the state registrations will become effective at the same time as, or after, the SEC registration becomes effective.

23. D: In business for a minimum of three years. The Notice filing method for registering a security with a state Administrator (also known as Registration by Notification or Registration by Filing) is only available to issuers that have been in business for at least three years, and who have a three-year history of filing records with Securities And Exchange Commission (SEC). This process is similar to Registration by Coordination, whereby security registration with both the SEC and state Administrators can be achieved without duplicating effort. The Notice filing method of registration cannot be used if the issuer has been in default for non-payment of any owed principal, interest or dividends at any time during the current fiscal year. The issuer must also meet additional minimum criteria for firm size net worth.

24. A: Registration by Filing process. The registration of a security filed by the Registration by Filing process, also called Registration by Notification, becomes effective at 3:00 p.m. Eastern Standard Time on the second business day after the request for registration is filed with the state Administrator. The state Administrator may order an earlier effective date. A registration does not become automatically effective if the Administrator issued a stop order (deny, suspend or revoke) or if a proceeding regarding the security's registration is currently pending.

25. C: A list of the issuer's competitors. The Registration by Qualification application requires the following information about the issuer of the security:

- The issuer's name and address
- The state or foreign country that has jurisdiction over the issuing entity
- The structure of the issuer's organization (e.g., corporation, limited partnerships, etc.)
- The incorporation date of the issuing entity
- Equipment and material property owned by the issuer
- A discussion of the competitive environment for the issuer's business

26. D: All of the above. The anti-fraud powers granted to the state Administrator by the Uniform Securities Act apply to all securities and securities transactions that occur within the state, and any and all fraudulent securities and their transactions are covered. This also includes securities exempt from registration, or ones registered with the Securities And Exchange Commission (SEC).

27. C: Securities issued as a private placement. Securities exempt from registration with the state Administrator include:

- Securities issued, guaranteed or insured by the United States, a state, a municipal government or a governmental body in Canada
- Securities issued or guaranteed by a bank, savings institution, trust company, savings and loan, building and loan, credit union or an international bank
- Securities issued or guaranteed by an insurance company to finance a debt and insurance company-offered stocks and bonds

- Securities issued by a utility or company governed by the Interstate Commerce Commission or the Public Utility Holding Company Act of 1935
- Federally covered securities
- Securities issued by non-profit organizations
- Investment contracts issued in connection with an employee benefit plan
- Securities issued as a promissory note worth a minimum $50,000 that receive one of the three highest possible ratings from a nationally recognized statistical rating firm

28. C: The National Securities Markets Improvement Act of 1996. The National Securities Markets Improvement Act of 1996 (NSMIA) established a clear division of responsibilities between state and federal regulators for the regulation of securities. NSMIA prohibits a state Administrator from regulating a security that is federally regulated, and state Administrators may not regulate securities that are regulated by the Securities And Exchange Commission. A security that is governed by federal regulations is called a federally covered security.

29. B: A person intentionally acting in a deceptive or misleading manner. The Uniform Securities Act (USA) prohibits fraudulent business practices. Fraud is the intentional act to deceive or mislead. Under the USA, other business practices are also prohibited, fraudulent or otherwise, to help protect the public from all types of unethical behavior,

30. D: Information that an investor relies upon when deciding whether or not to invest. The definition of a material fact is very broad, but is basically considered any piece of information an investor would consider in deciding whether or not to invest in a particular security. This would include information directly relating to the value of the security itself, or a statement by the Board of Directors, information contained in a prospectus, or even the experience and reputation of a broker-dealer, since the investor may rely on those variables when making an investment decision.

31. D: All of the above. The Uniform Securities Act prohibits fraud. Broker-dealers and agents cannot agree to perform services for clients knowing they're unable to do so, and cannot promise to provide a service to a client and not deliver that service. Additionally, omitting a material fact is called "fraud by omission," occurring when information likely to influence a client's investment decision, is not disclosed to that client. Broker-dealers and agents must also fully disclose to investors all transactions fees and commissions related to their work, as these are considered material facts. Intentionally not disclosing fees, as well as charges built into transactions as markups, is also fraud.

32. A: Facts that have not been made public that may impact the value of a security. The Uniform Securities Act prohibits persons from using material inside information to make investment recommendations. Inside information includes any facts, not currently public, that can potentially influence the value of a security. For example, an agent has a close relative who is negotiating a large contract with a publicly held company, and that relationship yields information to the agent that could affect the company's stock price. This information is considered material inside information; therefore, the agent must inform a supervisor of the information and is prohibited from making investment recommendations based on this information.

33. C: When the client offers securities loans as a regular part of business. The Uniform Securities Act (USA) has specific provisions placing limits on a security professional's ability to borrow from clients. As a general rule, securities professional are prohibited from borrowing either securities or funds from their clients. This behavior is considered unethical and is a USA violation. However, there are limited circumstances where borrowing is permissible:

- The client is a lending institution, such as a bank or saving and loan, that lends money as its normal course of business
- The client is a securities firm or other business that offers securities loans as its normal course of business

34. C: Backdating a record to correct an error in the original transaction. Backdating any of the records associated with a transaction is strictly prohibited, since such practices could be used to falsify the purchase or sale price of a security. The recording of all securities transactions, including private transactions, must be accurate, and handled in an ethical manner. This very broad requirement applies to other activities commonly performed in the retail brokerage community. Deliberately ignoring a client's instructions regarding the purchase or sale of securities is strictly prohibited, and client transactions must be accurately recorded in the broker-dealer's records unless the client has specifically requested in writing that the transaction not be recorded.

35. C: The markup was a clerical error. A clerical error does not constitute fraud because it was not an intentional act. The Uniform Securities Act prohibits the excessive markup of a security and is considered a fraudulent act when the person performing the markup intentionally attempts to mislead clients regarding the markup. For example, if a broker-dealer informs clients that a security has been marked up by one dollar, and the security has actually been marked up by two dollars, the broker-dealer has committed an act of fraud. Similarly, if a broker-dealer tries to convince its clients that a given markup is standard in the industry for the type of transaction in question, knowing it's excessive, the broker-dealer has committed fraud.

36. D: A guarantee of future performance of a security's principal return, dividends or interest. The Uniform Securities Act prohibits securities professionals from making guarantees related to the future performance of a security in terms of principal return, dividends or interest. It is, however, permitted to reference an existing guarantee applying to a security if a party other than the security's issuer has guaranteed the security in some way.

37. B: An artificial increase in the market value of a security. Matching purchases, a form of market manipulation, is prohibited by the Uniform Securities Act. Parties engaging in matching purchases are attempting to artificially increase the market value of a security by agreeing to repeatedly buy and sell the same security to increase its trading activity. This artificially high amount of activity has been known to entice investors to purchase shares and artificially increase the market value of the security. Once the market value of the security has increased, the parties engaging in the matching purchases then sell their shares at the artificially high price.

38. B: A written margin agreement. In addition to the standard requirement to obtain client authorization prior to engaging in a securities transaction, a broker-dealer must obtain an effective written margin agreement from clients wishing to open margin accounts. While the broker-dealer can initiate the first transaction in the client's margin account before it possesses an effective written margin agreement, the agreement must be obtained shortly after the initial transaction. Failure to obtain a margin agreement from the client in a timely manner may be grounds for a state Administrator to deny, suspend or revoke a broker-dealer's registration. Often, the margin agreement may accompany the account opening agreement.

39. D: Client-owned securities may not be placed in the broker-dealer's account. A broker-dealer must segregate client accounts appropriately; they may not place securities owned by a client in the firm's own account. Instead, client-owned securities must be placed in a separate client account. Broker-dealers must also segregate any free securities belonging to a client. Free securities are those in a margin account that are not used as collateral for the margin loan. A broker-dealer's failure to properly segregate client accounts may result in the denial, suspension, or revocation of the broker-dealer's license. The ethical management of all client accounts is a vital part of a broker-dealer's responsibilities.

40. D: 100%. A broker-dealer participating in a bona fide public offering must make its entire allotment available. This requirement applies whether the broker-dealer is an underwriter, a syndicate member, or acquired the shares from an underwriter or syndicate member. Also, the broker-dealer may not withhold distribution of a security that it has been entrusted to distribute. For example, a broker-dealer granted a specific allotment of securities for an IPO cannot hold the securities while waiting to see how high the price will climb. The broker-dealer must offer all of the securities in its allotment.

41. B: When the broker-dealers are affiliated with each other. A registered agent may represent multiple registered broker-dealers or issuers if all of those broker-dealers or issuers are affiliated with each other. To be considered an affiliate, each of the broker-dealers or issuers must have a common Controller. If the broker-dealers or issuers are not affiliated in this manner, an agent may still be permitted to represent them if the state Administrator gives authorization for the agent to operate under multiple licenses. Otherwise, an agent may only represent a single broker-dealer or issuer.

42. C: The amount of investment the client can afford. Agents must consider their clients' best interests when making investment recommendations. Before recommending securities, agents must obtain pertinent information from clients including current finances, investment goals and their need for investment stability. These three factors help the agent determine:

- The amount of investment the client can reasonably afford
- The types of securities that meet the client's investment goals
- The appropriate mix of high-risk and low-risk investments for the client

These client-driven factors must be integrated into any recommended securities transactions. The Uniform Securities Act prohibits agents from recommending an investment that is inconsistent with the client's investment objectives.

43. C: Verifiable facts. Investment recommendations to clients must be based on verifiable facts. This helps maintain an orderly market driven by actual performance, and not one manipulated by unfounded rumors. The Uniform Securities Act (USA) prohibits agents from making recommendations based on rumors, and from spreading rumors about securities. The USA cites penalties for rumor-based violations ranging from limiting an agent's securities activity to criminal prosecution.

44. B: When the agent has a joint account with the client. If an agent obtains prior written approval from a client and they jointly own the account, profits and losses for that account are shared and apportioned to each party based on percentage of ownership. An agent owning 15% of a joint account would be entitled to, or endure, 15% of the account's profits or losses. As a general rule, though, agents cannot share in a client's profits or losses, and broker-dealers are prohibited from establishing joint accounts with their clients.

45. D: When the investment adviser is legally ordered to release the information. Investment advisers are required to protect confidential client information and are prohibited from releasing information about a client's identity or the nature of the client's investment. The two exceptions are: (1) if the client authorizes the investment adviser to release the information to a third party, and (2) if the investment adviser is legally ordered to release the information through a subpoena. When legally ordered, the investment adviser must deliver only the information specified to the precise party indicated on the subpoena.

46. B: Provide written notification to the client. Investment advisers must provide written notification to clients of a conflict of interest before providing any investment advice related to the source of the conflict. A material conflict of interest could hinder the investment adviser's ability to provide objective and unbiased investment advice. A conflict of interest can occur when an investment adviser (or its employees) receives compensation from a source other than client fees (for example, a broker-dealer) for activities associated with the client's investments or securities transactions. Investment advisers, who collect advisory fees, must also provide written notification if it receives commission for transactions in addition to the fee.

47. D: When the Administrator has not ruled to prohibit custody. Investment advisers can maintain custody, which is possession or control, of a client's assets only under specific circumstances. Investment advisers may not maintain custody of client assets if the state Administrator issues a rule prohibiting such custody. The investment adviser is obligated to inform the Administrator when it has custody of a client's assets, and must provide regular statements (quarterly, at a minimum) to custodial clients specifying the value of the account, account transactions, and the location of all the client's assets.

48. B: The investment adviser is a financial institution. Investment advisers are generally prohibited from lending money to a client, as it is considered a conflict of interest. There are two exceptions to this provision: (1) Investment advisers are permitted to loan money to a client if the investment adviser is a financial institution, such as a bank, that loans money as a standard part of its business, and (2) investment advisers are permitted to loan money to clients that are affiliated with the investment adviser. Investment advisers are forbidden to loan any funds to any other clients. Such action is considered an unethical business practice and the investment adviser may have its registration denied, suspended, or revoked by the state Administrator.

49. B: Cannot promote their own interests above the interests of their clients. Investment advisers represent the clients, and as fiduciaries must place its clients' welfare above its own interests at all times. Although both broker-dealers and investment advisers are required to act ethically at all times, the fiduciary responsibilities of an investment adviser signify that clients' interests come ahead of their own. A broker-dealer could recommend that a client use the services of its firm for a particular securities transaction as long as the recommendation was made honestly and ethically; however, an investment adviser could not make the same recommendation if it was aware that the client could obtain a better deal by handling the transaction differently. While both the broker-dealer and the investment adviser acted ethically in this scenario, the broker-dealer represents itself, while the investment adviser must consider its fiduciary responsibility toward the client.

50. C: Before every transaction. Investment advisers must always obtain client authorization prior to every securities transaction. Investment advisers are prohibited from placing an order on behalf of a client to purchase and/or sell securities unless proper authorization from the client has been obtained. Although investment advisers are fiduciaries, an investment adviser may not transact business on the client's behalf without this authorization, even if the action would be in the best interest of the client. This procedure also applies to instances in which the investment adviser receives instructions to initiate a securities transaction from a third party. While it can accept the order, an investment adviser must have prior written authorization from the client to transact the order.

An investment adviser who initiates a client transaction without prior authorization may be penalized with the denial, revocation, or suspension of its registration.

51. D: Testimonials. The Uniform Securities Act limits the permissible content contained in an investment adviser's advertising. Testimonials are not permitted. Ann advertisement may contain information regarding the historical performance of recommended securities, but it must not limit the information only to successful recommendations. The content must include all of the recommendations the investment adviser made regarding the same type of securities during the past year, or longer. If historical performance is referenced, the advertisement must accurately reflect recommendations resulting in losses as well as those resulting in gains. The content rule applies to advertisements for both niche and mass audiences.

52. B: The name of the other party. An investment adviser who provides a report or recommendation to a client prepared by a third party must disclose the identity of that party. An investment adviser cannot take credit for someone else's work, but can use research performed by others to aid the investment adviser's own research efforts. In the course of planning client investment strategies, advisers who formulate their own research by utilizing published material are not obligated to disclose the author of the material they used.

53. B: To help enforce an out of state subpoena. An Administrator's investigative authority is not limited to the state over which the Administrator has jurisdiction; another state's Administrator may help in the enforcement of an out-of-state subpoena. Administrators have the authority to perform investigations necessary to ensure compliance with the Uniform Securities Act (USA). As part of this authority, an Administrator may issue subpoenas and require involved parties to produce relevant documentation and other evidence. An Administrator may require witnesses, some of whom may live out-of-state, to provide sworn testimony and affidavits regarding facts relevant to the investigation. This enables an Administrator to resolve complaints and effectively implement the USA's provisions. The results of an Administrator's investigation are public, but certain instance may warrant information remain private.

54. C: By issuing a cease-and-desist order. The Administrator has the ability to prevent anticipated violations of the Uniform Securities Act. If the Administrator believes that a violation is about to occur, a cease-and-desist order may be issued. A cease-and-desist order prohibits a specified party from engaging in a particular activity. The power to issue cease-and-desist orders enables the Administrator to pro-actively protect investors, instead of merely reacting after the violation has occurred. To enforce the order, the Administrator may have to petition the court to issue an injunction against the party. The Administrator is not required to hold a hearing prior to issuing a cease-and-desist order.

55. D: Any of the above. A securities transaction falls under a state Administrator's jurisdiction when it...

- originates in the Administrator's state
- is directed to the Administrator's state
- is accepted in the Administrator's state

The Uniform Securities Act is the source of the Administrator's jurisdiction, covering securities transactions and the persons performing those transactions in the Administrator's state. The Administrator has the power to adopt orders, issue rulings and subpoenas, and initiate and conduct investigations. In addition, the Administrator is responsible for managing the registrations for persons engaged in various securities transactions. The registration management duties of the Administrator include determining whether a party's registration should be approved, denied, suspended, or revoked.

56. B: One party extends an offer to transfer ownership of the security for an item of value. A security sale is any transaction in which the ownership of the security is transferred from one party to another for compensation, with such compensation not exclusively monetary. An item of value, such as a hard asset, comprises compensation and is considered a sale. The Administrator has jurisdiction over the sale of covered securities and other activities related to the sale. Regulated securities transactions also include those in which the seller offers a security as an incentive, or bonus, to encourage the sale of a non-security.

57. A: Issuing orders. An Administrator is permitted to issue a variety of orders that support its primary function of protecting investors and ensuring the public interest is served. The types of orders an Administrator can issue are denial, suspension, revocation, stop orders, and cease-and-desist orders. Each one impacts a person's right to conduct securities business within the state. Prior to issuing any order other than a cease-and-desist order, the Administrator must allow the other party an opportunity to present its case in a hearing. That party has 60 days to appeal orders affecting a license (denial, suspension and revocation orders).

58. D: Any of the above. The Administrator may choose to deny, suspend or revoke an applicant's registration if the applicant is not operating in accordance with the requirements of the Uniform Securities Act (USA). An applicant's failure to meet the minimum required financial standards may result in denial of registration, or if occurring after approval had been granted, either suspension or revocation of the registration. The Administrator may also take action to deny, suspend or revoke an applicant's registration if an applicant has intentionally violated any of the USA's provisions, or engaged in fraudulent or unethical securities practices.

59. D: The registrant is no longer considered a legal person. An Administrator may cancel a registration if it is determined that the registrant has ceased to exist (is no longer considered to be a legal person) or is no longer conducting business in the state. A cancelled registration is not grounds for a future denial, suspension or revocation of registration and does not carry a penalty. A registered party also has the option of withdrawing its own registration, without penalty, as long as the Administrator has not already initiated a proceeding to suspend or revoke the registration. Withdrawn registrations became effective 30 days after receipt of the withdrawal application, and a withdrawn registration does not preclude future registration.

60. D: A person must deliberately act in a manner designed to mislead. Providing false or misleading information in conjunction with a securities transaction is not sufficient to prove fraud has occurred. The activity is not considered fraudulent unless the person deliberately acted in a manner designed to mislead. If an agent informs a client that a merger was likely to occur, and probably increase the value of a particular investment in the near future, but the agent withholds information regarding significant hurdles to the completion of the merger, the withholding of the information is considered fraudulent. The statute of limitation for such criminal offenses under the Uniform Securities Act is five years and may carry a maximum penalty of $5,000 and/or up to three years in prison.

How to Overcome Test Anxiety

Just the thought of taking a test is enough to make most people a little nervous. A test is an important event that can have a long-term impact on your future, so it's important to take it seriously and it's natural to feel anxious about performing well. But just because anxiety is normal, that doesn't mean that it's helpful in test taking, or that you should simply accept it as part of your life. Anxiety can have a variety of effects. These effects can be mild, like making you feel slightly nervous, or severe, like blocking your ability to focus or remember even a simple detail.

If you experience test anxiety—whether severe or mild—it's important to know how to beat it. To discover this, first you need to understand what causes test anxiety.

Causes of Test Anxiety

While we often think of anxiety as an uncontrollable emotional state, it can actually be caused by simple, practical things. One of the most common causes of test anxiety is that a person does not feel adequately prepared for their test. This feeling can be the result of many different issues such as poor study habits or lack of organization, but the most common culprit is time management. Starting to study too late, failing to organize your study time to cover all of the material, or being distracted while you study will mean that you're not well prepared for the test. This may lead to cramming the night before, which will cause you to be physically and mentally exhausted for the test. Poor time management also contributes to feelings of stress, fear, and hopelessness as you realize you are not well prepared but don't know what to do about it.

Other times, test anxiety is not related to your preparation for the test but comes from unresolved fear. This may be a past failure on a test, or poor performance on tests in general. It may come from comparing yourself to others who seem to be performing better or from the stress of living up to expectations. Anxiety may be driven by fears of the future—how failure on this test would affect your educational and career goals. These fears are often completely irrational, but they can still negatively impact your test performance.

Elements of Test Anxiety

As mentioned earlier, test anxiety is considered to be an emotional state, but it has physical and mental components as well. Sometimes you may not even realize that you are suffering from test anxiety until you notice the physical symptoms. These can include trembling hands, rapid heartbeat, sweating, nausea, and tense muscles. Extreme anxiety may lead to fainting or vomiting. Obviously, any of these symptoms can have a negative impact on testing. It is important to recognize them as soon as they begin to occur so that you can address the problem before it damages your performance.

115

The mental components of test anxiety include trouble focusing and inability to remember learned information. During a test, your mind is on high alert, which can help you recall information and stay focused for an extended period of time. However, anxiety interferes with your mind's natural processes, causing you to blank out, even on the questions you know well. The strain of testing during anxiety makes it difficult to stay focused, especially on a test that may take several hours. Extreme anxiety can take a huge mental toll, making it difficult not only to recall test information but even to understand the test questions or pull your thoughts together.

Effects of Test Anxiety

Test anxiety is like a disease—if left untreated, it will get progressively worse. Anxiety leads to poor performance, and this reinforces the feelings of fear and failure, which in turn lead to poor performances on subsequent tests. It can grow from a mild nervousness to a crippling condition. If allowed to progress, test anxiety can have a big impact on your schooling, and consequently on your future.

Test anxiety can spread to other parts of your life. Anxiety on tests can become anxiety in any stressful situation, and blanking on a test can turn into panicking in a job situation. But fortunately, you don't have to let anxiety rule your testing and determine your grades. There are a number of relatively simple steps you can take to move past anxiety and function normally on a test and in the rest of life.

Physical Steps for Beating Test Anxiety

While test anxiety is a serious problem, the good news is that it can be overcome. It doesn't have to control your ability to think and remember information. While it may take time, you can begin taking steps today to beat anxiety.

Just as your first hint that you may be struggling with anxiety comes from the physical symptoms, the first step to treating it is also physical. Rest is crucial for having a clear, strong mind. If you are tired, it is much easier to give in to anxiety. But if you establish good sleep habits, your body and mind will be ready to perform optimally, without the strain of exhaustion. Additionally, sleeping well helps you to retain information better, so you're more likely to recall the answers when you see the test questions.

Getting good sleep means more than going to bed on time. It's important to allow your brain time to relax. Take study breaks from time to time so it doesn't get overworked, and don't study right before bed. Take time to rest your mind before trying to rest your body, or you may find it difficult to fall asleep.

Along with sleep, other aspects of physical health are important in preparing for a test. Good nutrition is vital for good brain function. Sugary foods and drinks may give a burst of energy but this burst is followed by a crash, both physically and emotionally. Instead, fuel your body with protein and vitamin-rich foods.

116

Also, drink plenty of water. Dehydration can lead to headaches and exhaustion, especially if your brain is already under stress from the rigors of the test. Particularly if your test is a long one, drink water during the breaks. And if possible, take an energy-boosting snack to eat between sections.

Along with sleep and diet, a third important part of physical health is exercise. Maintaining a steady workout schedule is helpful, but even taking 5-minute study breaks to walk can help get your blood pumping faster and clear your head. Exercise also releases endorphins, which contribute to a positive feeling and can help combat test anxiety.

When you nurture your physical health, you are also contributing to your mental health. If your body is healthy, your mind is much more likely to be healthy as well. So take time to rest, nourish your body with healthy food and water, and get moving as much as possible. Taking these physical steps will make you stronger and more able to take the mental steps necessary to overcome test anxiety.

Mental Steps for Beating Test Anxiety

Working on the mental side of test anxiety can be more challenging, but as with the physical side, there are clear steps you can take to overcome it. As mentioned earlier, test anxiety often stems from lack of preparation, so the obvious solution is to prepare for the test. Effective studying may be the most important weapon you have for beating test anxiety, but you can and should employ several other mental tools to combat fear.

First, boost your confidence by reminding yourself of past success—tests or projects that you aced. If you're putting as much effort into preparing for this test as you did for those, there's no reason you should expect to fail here. Work hard to prepare; then trust your preparation.

Second, surround yourself with encouraging people. It can be helpful to find a study group, but be sure that the people you're around will encourage a positive attitude. If you spend time with others who are anxious or cynical, this will only contribute to your own anxiety. Look for others who are motivated to study hard from a desire to succeed, not from a fear of failure.

Third, reward yourself. A test is physically and mentally tiring, even without anxiety, and it can be helpful to have something to look forward to. Plan an activity following the test, regardless of the outcome, such as going to a movie or getting ice cream.

When you are taking the test, if you find yourself beginning to feel anxious, remind yourself that you know the material. Visualize successfully completing the test. Then take a few deep, relaxing breaths and return to it. Work through the questions carefully but with confidence, knowing that you are capable of succeeding.

Developing a healthy mental approach to test taking will also aid in other areas of life. Test anxiety affects more than just the actual test—it can be damaging to your

117

mental health and even contribute to depression. It's important to beat test anxiety before it becomes a problem for more than testing.

Study Strategy

Being prepared for the test is necessary to combat anxiety, but what does being prepared look like? You may study for hours on end and still not feel prepared. What you need is a strategy for test prep. The next few pages outline our recommended steps to help you plan out and conquer the challenge of preparation.

STEP 1: SCOPE OUT THE TEST

Learn everything you can about the format (multiple choice, essay, etc.) and what will be on the test. Gather any study materials, course outlines, or sample exams that may be available. Not only will this help you to prepare, but knowing what to expect can help to alleviate test anxiety.

STEP 2: MAP OUT THE MATERIAL

Look through the textbook or study guide and make note of how many chapters or sections it has. Then divide these over the time you have. For example, if a book has 15 chapters and you have five days to study, you need to cover three chapters each day. Even better, if you have the time, leave an extra day at the end for overall review after you have gone through the material in depth.

If time is limited, you may need to prioritize the material. Look through it and make note of which sections you think you already have a good grasp on, and which need review. While you are studying, skim quickly through the familiar sections and take more time on the challenging parts. Write out your plan so you don't get lost as you go. Having a written plan also helps you feel more in control of the study, so anxiety is less likely to arise from feeling overwhelmed at the amount to cover.

STEP 3: GATHER YOUR TOOLS

Decide what study method works best for you. Do you prefer to highlight in the book as you study and then go back over the highlighted portions? Or do you type out notes of the important information? Or is it helpful to make flashcards that you can carry with you? Assemble the pens, index cards, highlighters, post-it notes, and any other materials you may need so you won't be distracted by getting up to find things while you study.

If you're having a hard time retaining the information or organizing your notes, experiment with different methods. For example, try color-coding by subject with colored pens, highlighters, or post-it notes. If you learn better by hearing, try recording yourself reading your notes so you can listen while in the car, working out, or simply sitting at your desk. Ask a friend to quiz you from your flashcards, or try teaching someone the material to solidify it in your mind.

STEP 4: CREATE YOUR ENVIRONMENT

It's important to avoid distractions while you study. This includes both the obvious distractions like visitors and the subtle distractions like an uncomfortable chair (or a too-comfortable couch that makes you want to fall asleep). Set up the best study environment possible: good lighting and a comfortable work area. If background music helps you focus, you may want to turn it on, but otherwise keep the room quiet. If you are using a computer to take notes, be sure you don't have any other windows open, especially applications like social media, games, or anything else that could distract you. Silence your phone and turn off notifications. Be sure to keep water close by so you stay hydrated while you study (but avoid unhealthy drinks and snacks).

Also, take into account the best time of day to study. Are you freshest first thing in the morning? Try to set aside some time then to work through the material. Is your mind clearer in the afternoon or evening? Schedule your study session then. Another method is to study at the same time of day that you will take the test, so that your brain gets used to working on the material at that time and will be ready to focus at test time.

STEP 5: STUDY!

Once you have done all the study preparation, it's time to settle into the actual studying. Sit down, take a few moments to settle your mind so you can focus, and begin to follow your study plan. Don't give in to distractions or let yourself procrastinate. This is your time to prepare so you'll be ready to fearlessly approach the test. Make the most of the time and stay focused.

Of course, you don't want to burn out. If you study too long you may find that you're not retaining the information very well. Take regular study breaks. For example, taking five minutes out of every hour to walk briskly, breathing deeply and swinging your arms, can help your mind stay fresh.

As you get to the end of each chapter or section, it's a good idea to do a quick review. Remind yourself of what you learned and work on any difficult parts. When you feel that you've mastered the material, move on to the next part. At the end of your study session, briefly skim through your notes again.

But while review is helpful, cramming last minute is NOT. If at all possible, work ahead so that you won't need to fit all your study into the last day. Cramming overloads your brain with more information than it can process and retain, and your tired mind may struggle to recall even previously learned information when it is overwhelmed with last-minute study. Also, the urgent nature of cramming and the stress placed on your brain contribute to anxiety. You'll be more likely to go to the test feeling unprepared and having trouble thinking clearly.

So don't cram, and don't stay up late before the test, even just to review your notes at a leisurely pace. Your brain needs rest more than it needs to go over the information again. In fact, plan to finish your studies by noon or early afternoon the day before the test. Give your brain the rest of the day to relax or focus on other things, and get a good night's sleep. Then you will be fresh for the test and better able to recall what you've studied.

STEP 6: TAKE A PRACTICE TEST

Many courses offer sample tests, either online or in the study materials. This is an excellent resource to check whether you have mastered the material, as well as to prepare for the test format and environment.

Check the test format ahead of time: the number of questions, the type (multiple choice, free response, etc.), and the time limit. Then create a plan for working through them. For example, if you have 30 minutes to take a 60-question test, your limit is 30 seconds per question. Spend less time on the questions you know well so that you can take more time on the difficult ones.

If you have time to take several practice tests, take the first one open book, with no time limit. Work through the questions at your own pace and make sure you fully understand them. Gradually work up to taking a test under test conditions: sit at a desk with all study materials put away and set a timer. Pace yourself to make sure you finish the test with time to spare and go back to check your answers if you have time.

After each test, check your answers. On the questions you missed, be sure you understand why you missed them. Did you misread the question (tests can use tricky wording)? Did you forget the information? Or was it something you hadn't learned? Go back and study any shaky areas that the practice tests reveal.

Taking these tests not only helps with your grade, but also aids in combating test anxiety. If you're already used to the test conditions, you're less likely to worry about it, and working through tests until you're scoring well gives you a confidence boost. Go through the practice tests until you feel comfortable, and then you can go into the test knowing that you're ready for it.

Test Tips

On test day, you should be confident, knowing that you've prepared well and are ready to answer the questions. But aside from preparation, there are several test day strategies you can employ to maximize your performance.

First, as stated before, get a good night's sleep the night before the test (and for several nights before that, if possible). Go into the test with a fresh, alert mind rather than staying up late to study.

Try not to change too much about your normal routine on the day of the test. It's important to eat a nutritious breakfast, but if you normally don't eat breakfast at all, consider eating just a protein bar. If you're a coffee drinker, go ahead and have your normal coffee. Just make sure you time it so that the caffeine doesn't wear off right in the middle of your test. Avoid sugary beverages, and drink enough water to stay hydrated but not so much that you need a restroom break 10 minutes into the test. If your test isn't first thing in the morning, consider going for a walk or doing a light workout before the test to get your blood flowing.

Allow yourself enough time to get ready, and leave for the test with plenty of time to spare so you won't have the anxiety of scrambling to arrive in time. Another reason to be early is to select a good seat. It's helpful to sit away from doors and windows, which can be distracting. Find a good seat, get out your supplies, and settle your mind before the test begins.

When the test begins, start by going over the instructions carefully, even if you already know what to expect. Make sure you avoid any careless mistakes by following the directions.

Then begin working through the questions, pacing yourself as you've practiced. If you're not sure on an answer, don't spend too much time on it, and don't let it shake your confidence. Either skip it and come back later, or eliminate as many wrong answers as possible and guess among the remaining ones. Don't dwell on these questions as you continue—put them out of your mind and focus on what lies ahead.

Be sure to read all of the answer choices, even if you're sure the first one is the right answer. Sometimes you'll find a better one if you keep reading. But don't second-guess yourself if you do immediately know the answer. Your gut instinct is usually right. Don't let test anxiety rob you of the information you know.

If you have time at the end of the test (and if the test format allows), go back and review your answers. Be cautious about changing any, since your first instinct tends to be correct, but make sure you didn't misread any of the questions or accidentally mark the wrong answer choice. Look over any you skipped and make an educated guess.

At the end, leave the test feeling confident. You've done your best, so don't waste time worrying about your performance or wishing you could change anything. Instead, celebrate the successful completion of this test. And finally, use this test to learn how to deal with anxiety even better next time.

> **Review Video: Test Anxiety**
> Visit mometrix.com/academy and enter code: 100340

Important Qualification

Not all anxiety is created equal. If your test anxiety is causing major issues in your life beyond the classroom or testing center, or if you are experiencing troubling physical symptoms related to your anxiety, it may be a sign of a serious physiological or psychological condition. If this sounds like your situation, we strongly encourage you to seek professional help.

Additional Bonus Material

Due to our efforts to try to keep this book to a manageable length, we've created a link that will give you access to all of your additional bonus material:

mometrix.com/bonus948/series63